Organizations, Management, and Control

ORGANIZATIONS, MANAGEMENT,

RUSSELL STOUT, JR.

AND CONTROL

AN ANNOTATED BIBLIOGRAPHY

INDIANA UNIVERSITY PRESS

BLOOMINGTON

Manufactured in the United States of America

Library of Congress Cataloging in Publication Data

Stout, Russell, Jr. 1932-
Organizations, management, and control.

Includes index.
1. Management—Bibliography.   2. Organization—
Bibliography.   I. Title.
Z7164.C81S779 [HD31]   016.6584   79-3639
ISBN 0-253-14448-5   1 2 3 4 5 84 83 82 81 80

This book was written with support from the Midwest Universities
Consortium for International Activities' Program of Advanced Studies
in Institution Building and Technical Assistance Methodology
(PASITAM), which is funded by a grant from the Development Support
Bureau (RAD), U.S. Agency for International Development. Contractors
undertaking projects under government sponsorship are encouraged to
express their professional judgment freely in the conduct of the project.
Points of view or opinions stated do not, therefore, necessarily represent
the official AID position or policy.

Contents

Developing Countries   77

Evaluation   94

Management   100

Organization   131

Acknowledgments

At some point, preparing a bibliography stops being fun. After the reading is done there are the hard decisions and the checking and rechecking of citations, sources, and classifications. It is not a job for one person; the task demands the cooperation and patience of a lot of people. Too many of those who helped on this project cannot be listed. But there are some who deserve more acknowledgment than I can adequately provide here.

Richard A. Steele was my unflagging adviser and collaborator in surveying the literature and developing and refining the categories. He and his staff at the International Development Institute made many trips to the library to make sure our index cards were accurate. Marianne K. Platt did the editing and design. She also provided the friendly criticism and commiseration needed to get this into print. Barbara Dutton and her team did what seemed to be the endless typing and retyping. I know how tedious it was, and I hope my appreciation helped make it easier.

As always, Bill Siffin's wise counsel and encouragement was invaluable in keeping the work moving and on track.

Thank you all.

A Perspective on the Problem

The Problem

There is a pervasive confusion of the concepts of management and control in the organization and management (O&M) literature and in the instruction given students in schools of business and public administration. We equate management with control, and the terms are often used synonymously. Yet control has a specific meaning: a capacity to determine events, or to influence them so that they are determined. This presumes a high degree of predictability and more than a passive expectation of a specific outcome. Managing, on the other hand, denotes an ability to handle unpredictable events and outcomes that can only be influenced at the margin.

The distinction between management and control is no mere semantic quibble. It influences the way we define and solve problems. Our actions have real-world repercussions, and mistaking management for control affects nature and events. There is an intuitive understanding of this in ordinary usage. We speak, for example, of *managing* our environment and natural resources, because we know we cannot *control* them. Our everyday language, therefore, acknowledges the critical distinguishing property of management and control as the connotation each has in relation to uncertainty. An obvious indication of this can be found in the etymology of the two words.

The verb "to manage" comes from the Italian "maneggiare," which originally referred to training horses, i.e., making seemingly random conduct more predictable. Trainers constantly make implicit, probabilistic calculations of their animals' behavior. And although animals can be trained to perfection (as the Lippizaner horse troop), we are never completely sure they will perform as advertised. The uncertainty inherent in the enterprise provides the audience appeal and the trainer's challenge. There is little audience for mechanical lions and tigers jumping through hoops or clockwork horses performing perfect paces.

The verb "to control" is from the Old French "contre role," or "counter roll," i.e., a written record of financial transactions (as at a cashier's cage) that is a check on dishonesty and inaccurate calculations. Counter rolls significantly reduce the lurking uncertainty associated with cash computations. In such situations, the boundaries are quite clear and the methods are known. Since the problem is technical, disagreement invariably equals error. Accounting and accountability come from the same root and share the connotation of reducing discretion and uncertainty.

The distinction between management and control is the same as the distinction we make between development and production. Problems of development arise in the absence of a proven technology or an acceptable value agreement. Production problems, however, are a result of gaps in knowledge, technical malfunctions, or minor disagreements in an otherwise well-developed value consensus.

Production functions are essentially programmed. Problems that arise are usually minor digressions from an otherwise known and agreed-upon strategy. Control, therefore, is suitable for production. Technology exists, agreement has been reached, and control systems can and should be used to maintain progress on the proper path. These are the assembly line or accounting and payroll operations that lend themselves to sensible handling "as if" they were certain. Problems do arise, but they are usually disposed of rather quickly. If a problem persists and if a solution or resolution eludes us, then it is not a production problem; we are not past the development stage.

There is a lesson in this for organizational actions. When we fuse the concepts of management and control, we leave no term for the vast majority of organizational circumstances that by their very nature are not under control. Most organizational problems fall into this category. A condition that is under control is not problematical, and the skills required can be reduced to a program. But management requires imagination, craft, understanding, and patience. If the terms management and control are to have meaning, then we must map a domain of tasks and circumstances that call for managing and may eventually be subject to control.[1]

The distinction between management and control is easiest understood as a continuum of risk, from certainty at one end to uncertainty at the other.

CERTAINTY ————————————————————— UNCERTAINTY

RISK

We know that perfect examples of either condition are not found in nature, so we grade the various points along the continuum in terms of probabilities. These distributions are calculated as either *objective* or *subjective* probabilities.

| Objective | Subjective |
| Probability | Probability |

CERTAINTY ————————————————————— UNCERTAINTY

RISK

Objective probabilities are evaluated by empirical observation, and the likelihood of certain outcomes can be reliably calculated and predicted. Games of chance like fair coin or dice tosses are familiar examples; we don't know what the next toss will bring, but time and experience permit us to compute the probability (odds) of each outcome, given a finite range of alternatives. Once calculated, objective probabilities are tested against results; and although we cannot control the event (heads or tails), we organize our actions *as if* we could and develop strategies to control other conditions.

As we move toward uncertainty, however, we depend on belief to assign probability. These "subjective probabilities have all the mathematical properties of objective probabilities except that they are unique to the individual."[2] Subjective probabilities are educated guesses, those vague hunches about what we should do. They do not depend on an empirical outcome (though they can), and are assigned on the basis of confidence. This is perfectly acceptable because in the absence of perfect knowledge we have no alternative.

---

1. For more on this subject, see Russell Stout, Jr., *Management or Control? The Organizational Challenge* (Bloomington: Indiana University Press, 1980).

2. Sheen Kassouf, *Normative Decision Making* (Englewood Cliffs, N.J.: Prentice-Hall, 1970), p. 46.

But we deal with subjective probabilities at the risk of unforeseen error. In these relatively uncertain areas, we manage; that is, we acknowledge the character of the circumstance and remain sensitive to the likelihood of error. We may not gain enough knowledge to move to objective probability, but there is no reason to assume *a priori* that we will not.

The utility of viewing management and control along a risk continuum can be further illustrated by situating organizational activities on the continuum and linking these to modern management techniques and practices. This emphasizes the heuristic appeal of the continuum. To be sure, any placing is tentative and subject to revision as more knowledge is gained.

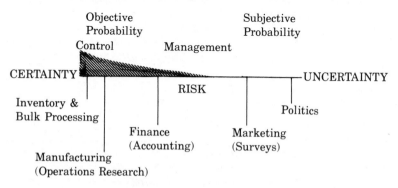

Control is only possible at the left end of the continuum. But there are activities that are close enough to be handled as if they were governed by objective probabilities. Product storage and inventory, quality control, and bulk materials processing are examples. These operations take place within the larger uncertainties of material availability, marketing, and social interactions. This overlap of control and management is typical of a good deal of organizational activities. But as we move away from the control and overlap area, management as a conscious strategy becomes paramount.

Obviously, at some point (for convenience, I have placed it at the middle) control is impossible, and routines that serve well even in the overlap area are no longer useful. Forcing control methods in such circumstances leads to disaster, since situations are then completely mishandled. But as knowledge (probability calculation) is refined, the activity could be moved to the control/management realm.

Management, of course, calls for strategies and modes of action different from control. Since outcomes are not predictable, there must be adequate margin for error detection and correction, and this calls for flexible, adaptive responses to problems. As risk increases, we are forced into subjective responses, and "the demands on the decision maker are more severe when working with subjective probabilities."[3] Programmed reactions to unprogrammed situations are unsuitable, because the looseness that could produce resiliency is designed out of the system. The major risk in working with subjective probabilities is that subjective certainty will be exhibited in the face of objective uncertainty; we accept as fact the hypotheses or myths proposed to deal with development.

The Perspective

The distinction between management and control and the continuum of risk running from certainty to uncertainty guided the classification scheme of the bibliography. An understanding of this perspective should ease the way through the annotations. The categories are in part limited by the self-defining properties of the literature. Of the eleven major categories, a few fall into that class. Computers and information are almost always paired nowadays. It seemed prudent to retain that grouping. Some sections, such as Control, Decision, Managing, and Organization speak for themselves. But other labels are not so obvious. Briefly, this is how they have been classified:

Accounting and Budgeting. The inherent properties of accounting and budgeting usually go unrecognized. Both are assumed to be objective, number-crunching activities, when in fact they are highly political and subjective. Both are usually presented as epitomizing the control principle, yet they are essentially managing functions. Efforts to cram accounting and budgeting into closed system strategies (PPB, for example) inevitably collapse because they are designed with scant attention paid to the dynamics of resource allocation and managing.

We attribute authority to accountants partly because they are the ones who seem to know what's going on. They have the information about the balance sheet, about what's profitable and what isn't. And they know the arcane secrets of taxes, costs, and manipulating double-entry bookkeeping. By virtue of accountants' access to the esoteric, and because they handle our finances, we stand

---

3. Ibid.

in awe of the accounting process and its outcomes. In fact, as a student of the profession has pointed out: "Accounting and its effectiveness can be understood much better from a psychological than from a logical point of view. . . . The effectiveness of traditional accounting lies not in the preciseness of information to management for maximizing profits or any other entrepreneurial goal, but in its authoritative character."[4] So it is with budgeting as well; the outcome becomes imbued with a formally rational authority that is not consistent with the ambiguity that characterizes the process.

Analytical Methods and Quantitative Techniques. Many of the methods discussed in this section are treated with the same awe that is attached to accounting and budgeting. Part of the reason for this is the modern preoccupation with numbers and the precision we associate with their manipulation. But numbers are used to hide as well as to disclose truth. A case could be made for the argument that many quantitative techniques serve better as political ploys to attack or defend programs than as scientific, analytical tools. This is not to condemn the utility of modern economic and management science approaches, but only to sound a caveat about their unlimited extension to uncertain domains for which they were not designed.

Developing Countries. A section on developing countries is included because the problems of economic and social development have attracted pretenders who claim that management science and its techniques are a panacea. Third World nations are forced to deal with the natural uncertainties that face us all; they must also cope with a world economy that is influenced only by their most extraordinary actions. The articles and books in this section present a varied picture of attempts to install industrial methods in essentially agrarian societies. Not all the efforts have been failures, and the distinction between management and control helps us to understand what might succeed and why.

Evaluation. This category contains material on applying social science statistical methods to the evaluation of organizations and social programs. The approach is a partial response to the need for accountability in organizational actions. The literature ranges from the banal to the insightful. I have minimized the technical debates and have concentrated instead on materials that discuss

---

4. R. Matessich, *Accounting and Analytical Methods* (London: Irwin, 1964), pp. 413-14.

the utility of methods and the feasibility of evaluation as a profession and a discipline.

Planning and Policy. These subjects receive a great deal of attention in the O&M literature and the popular press. They are presented as technical enterprises, entirely suitable to the application of conceptual gadgets planners and policy analysts just happen to know about. Lost in the technical jargon is the essential political character of organizations and the overwhelming need for flexibility and pragmatism in preparing for the future. Planning is hypothesis development and policy is hypothesis testing. Unless this is recognized, chaos and frustration are not far away.

R.E.D. (Gene) Woolsey. Finally, Gene Woolsey is placed in a separate category because this marvelous iconoclast deserves it. His sage snipings at his own profession are a delight to read and think about. Managers are ill-served by the limited availability of his work. He warrants a wider audience, and I hope this effort helps to bring his thinking to the attention of more people.

The ten major categories (Woolsey is the eleventh) are further divided to simplify locating subjects and materials. Full title, author, and source are included for each entry. In addition, cross-references to related sub-categories are provided. Finally, of course, each entry is annotated.

The sub-categories provide a more detailed specification for the article or book. Thus, the item is placed in context for comparison with similar publications. The cross-reference enables the reader to either further investigate the subject or to gain a broader perspective on the literature in related areas.

The entry below illustrates how the elements are presented:

Major category	**Analytical Methods and Quantitative Techniques**
Sub-category	**ANALYTICAL METHODS**
Author, title, source	Brewer, Garry D. "What's the Purpose? What's the Use? A Review of a Management Science Special Issue on 'Urban Issues'." *Interfaces* 4 (February 1974):60-74.
Cross-reference	**Evaluation and program effectiveness, Management in public organizations.**
Annotation	An intelligent review that stands as an original essay on management science techniques by one of the more pragmatic people in the field.

Entries of particular worth are identified as *Recommended* or *Highly Recommended* after the annotation. In some cases I did this to highlight the seminal, well-known works. In others, the label points out an original contribution that has been ignored or glossed over.

An Editorial Note

This collection will interest managers and students of organizations and management. It is based on an exhaustive and systematic examination of books, professional academic journals, and popular periodicals available throughout the world. The stacks of books and articles that appear each year purporting to tell us all we've ever wanted to know about management are generally dull, if not misleading and occasionally downright wrong. Discerning readers quickly realize this, but not until they have bought the book or read the article. By spending time and money on these materials, we tell publishers that there is a market for printed imposture.

To guide managers through this maze of pretension, I offer a partial mapping of the O&M literature. The map is partial because, although the search was extensive, I have intentionally or inadvertently omitted a good deal of material. The articles and books included are what I consider the most representative of a diverse body of knowledge. So this book is not a listing of the "best of" the O&M publications. The selection process was eclectic and idiosyncratic and reflects my own judgment and familiarity with the literature. Through sheer physical necessity, my search was restricted to the ten-year period 1969-79. Obvious exceptions are the classic works of F.W. Taylor, Henri Fayol, Chester Barnard, Herbert A. Simon, and others. Where an item predating 1969 is included, it serves a specific purpose and is explained in the annotation.

I have long thought it necessary for serious students of organizations to address the problems of practicing managers. The early management thinker's intense interest in task accomplishment partially explains why their "principles" persist. Although some of their work is now anachronistic, the classical concern with *work*, with getting things done, is still valid. Modern scholars need to become involved in administration, in management, and in the problems of control. By exchanging ideas and experiences, academics and professional managers enhance our understanding of organizations and management. And only through improved understanding can we have better managed organizations.

Organizations, Management, and Control

Accounting and Budgeting

ACCOUNTING

Gambling, Trevor. "Magic, Accounting and Morale." *Accounting, Organizations and Society* 2 (1977):141-51. **Control systems and techniques, Organization and management theory, Risk and uncertainty.**

A delight! One of the most astute, insightful, and readable statements on the functional *use* of accounting in modern organizations. Gambling gives an excellent view of management tasks (p. 147). **Recommended.**

Ledbetter, J. Lee, and Bowker, Robert M. "AIM." *Financial Executive* 46 (October 1978):44-55. **Control systems and techniques, Organizational growth and change.**

Formalistic, prescriptive control nonsense. This *may* have made sense to F. W. Taylor, but given current organizational knowledge, it's a waste of time and effort.

MacKay, A. E. "Management Control in a Changing Environment." *Financial Executive* 47 (March 1979):25-33. **Control systems and techniques, Organizational growth and change.**

A formal discussion of accounting internal control procedures. Of marginal interest and utility.

Matessich, Richard. *Accounting and Analytical Methods*. Homewood, Ill.: Richard D. Irwin, 1964. **Analytical methods, Operations research and management science.**

I have not examined every book on accounting, but it is hard to imagine a better discussion of the relation of accounting to business, economics, operations research and management science, and everyday life. This is a lucid explanation of some very difficult concepts and methods. **Recommended.**

McGrail, George R. "The Decision Making Process in Small Businesses." *Managerial Planning* (January-February 1978), pp. 19-25. **Control systems and techniques, Decisionmaking.**

A short outline of accounting uses in small business. The author assumes the classic, formally rational decisionmaking process accurately reflects reality.

McRae, T. W. "The Behavioral Critique of Accounting." *Accounting and Business Research,* no. 2 (Spring 1971), pp. 83-92. **Organizational growth and change, Organization and management theory.**

A summary of the arguments (primarily socio-psychological) that criticize accounting and related control systems. The author is not defensive or hysterical; he just gives us the facts.

Myklebust, Harold N. "Human Resource Performance: Management Control Through Accounting Feedback." *Government Accountants Journal* 25 (Summer 1976):52-60. **Personnel management, Control systems and techniques.**

The accountant ascendant. Despite serious questions raised by others in the profession, the author sees accounting practices extended into controlling all organizational resources.

AUDITING

Culbertson, Roy C. "How Computers Affect Auditing." *Internal Auditor* 33 (February 1978):53-57. **Accounting, Computer services.**

Interesting views of an internal auditor who asks some good, hard questions about the universal utility of computerized accounting systems.

George, Frank F., and Palmer, Frederick B. "Systems Auditability and Control." *Internal Auditor* 34 (April 1977):11-15. **Computer services, Electronic data processing.**

Not a significant statement, but there are some interesting expressions of disquiet on the auditability of data processing systems. It seems that EDP applications are ahead of the auditors. This is not a good sign if accountability is needed.

Hershman, Arlene. "The GAO: Watching Over Washington." *Dun's Review* 111 (February 1977):38-43. **Evaluation, Management in public organizations.**

A good profile of the U.S. Government Accounting Office (GAO), Hershman illustrates how evaluation can accumulate power and make enemies.

Mautz, Robert K., and White, Bernard J. "Internal Control: A Management View." *Financial Executive* 47 (June 1979):12-18. **Control systems and techniques, Accounting.**

A narrow account of how to install internal audit controls. This is typical of accounting's control orientation.

McCurry, Charles M. "Top Management Talks About the Audit Function." *Magazine of Bank Administration* 52 (October 1976):36-39. **Managerial functions.**

A cursory review of executive responses to a questionnaire on the audit function. This is hardly worth the trouble.

Morse, Ellsworth H., Jr. "Relationship Between Internal Auditors and Independent Auditors." *GAO Review* 9 (Winter 1974):25-31. **Management in public organizations, Control systems and techniques.**

A short piece with some interesting information on the General Accounting Office's (GAO) view of auditing.

Richardson, Dana R. "Auditing EFTS: How the Auditor Should View the Client's EFTS in Light of Internal Controls." *Journal of Accountancy* (October 1978), pp. 81-87. **Electronic data processing, Information management.**

One of the better examinations of the problems to be dealt with as more electronic funds transfer (EFT) systems are installed and "interfaced."

BUDGETING

Keown, Arthur J., and Martin, John D. "Capital Budgeting in the Public Sector: A Zero-One Goal Programming Approach." *Financial Management* 7 (Summer 1978):21-27. **Management in public organizations.**

A simplistic quantitative method of resolving budgeting conflict in multi-goal circumstances. All you need is agreement on priorities — simple.

Klammer, Thomas. "Empirical Evidence of the Adoption of Sophisticated Capital Budgeting Techniques." *Journal of Business* 45 (July 1972):387-97. **Analytical methods, Managerial functions.**

This study (in 1970) found that payback was the method most often used in capital budgeting decisions. The author predicts that more sophisticated techniques will come into use, but this is not borne out in later studies.

Mehler, Edmund W. "Capital Budgeting: Theory and Practice." *Management Accounting* 58 (September 1976):32-38. **Analytical methods, Policymaking.**

Another indication that pay-back is the method most often used in reaching capital investment decisions. Cost-benefit is down the list.

MANAGEMENT ACCOUNTING

Clancy, Donald K. "The Management Control Problems of Responsibility Accounting." *Management Accounting* 59 (March 1978):35-39. **Control systems and techniques, Organizational goals and objectives.**

A typical example of the management/control confusion. Clancy implicitly recognizes the distinction but assumes that all is subsumed by control.

Davis, James R. "EDP Control Means Total Control." *Management Accounting* 58 (January 1977):41-44. **Organizational learning, Electronic data processing.**

A review of the significant differences in manual and automated accounting systems. Davis gives us nothing new or startling, but he presents some interesting caveats.

Gambling, Trevor. *Societal Accounting*. London: Allen & Unwin, 1974. **Policy analysis, Analytical methods.**

This is an interesting though too often obscure book. Gambling's goal is ambitious and unrealized, but getting there is a provocative if somewhat frustrating quest.

Hayes, David C. "The Contingency Theory of Managerial Accounting." *Accounting Review* 52 (January 1977):22-37. **Analytical methods, Organization and management theory.**

Rather hard going, but this is a good empirical investigation of managerial accounting and organizational subunit performance. The author concludes that accounting systems that focus on cost data are not good universal measures of performance.

Hopwood, A. G. "Problems with Using Accounting Information in Performance Evaluation." *Management International Review* 13 (1973):83-91. **Managerial functions, Performance appraisal.**

A study of accounting systems and their use and misuse by managers. This is a much ignored area that requires further research.

Judelson, David N. "Financial Controls That Work." *Financial Executive* 45 (January 1977):22-25. **Control systems and techniques, Planning.**

Another list of "dos" and "don'ts" in financial control systems. Not very useful.

MacLellan, R. P. "A Company Director's View of Accountants." *Accountants Magazine* 77 (September 1973):486-89. **Accounting.**

A tongue-in-cheek view of accountants and their profession. The points are well-made, even if buried in some bad puns and asides.

PLANNING, PROGRAMMING, AND BUDGETING

Bickner, Robert E. "I Don't Know PPB at All." *Policy Sciences* 2 (1971):301-304. **Planning, Decisionmaking.**

A short but cogent statement on problems with Planning-Programming-Budgeting (PPB).

Hatry, Harry P. "Status of PPBS in Local and State Governments in the U.S." *Policy Sciences* 2 (June 1971):177-89. **Management in public organizations, Control systems and techniques.**

An out-of-date update on PPB.

Jablonsky, Stephen F., and Dirsmith, Mark W. "The Pattern of PPB Rejection: Something About Organizations, Something About PPB." *Accounting, Organizations and Society* 3 (1978):215-25. **Budgeting, Control systems and techniques.**

A bit muddled, but a good, reasonable attempt at a "pathological study of PPB failure." Conclusion: PPB guaranteed the wrong decision for the context in which it was used. PPB is analyzed as a decision strategy.

Lyden, Fremont J., and Miller, Ernest G., eds. *Planning, Programming, Budgeting: A Systems Approach to Management.* 2d ed. Chicago: Markham, 1972. **Budgeting, Control systems and techniques.**

One of the better readers on the subject. The PPB experience must be reexamined with the zero-base budgeting scheme in mind. The basic premise behind both movements is similar.

ZERO-BASE BUDGETING

Anderson, Donald N. "Zero-Base Budgeting: How to Get Rid of Corporate Crabgrass." *Management Review* 65 (October 1976):4-17. **Evaluation and program effectiveness, Analytical methods.**

A formal statement of how ZBOP (Zero-Base Operational Planning and Budgeting) saved a utility company. Lots of claims with no evidence.

―――. "Ingredients for Successful Zero-Based Budgeting Implementation (Advice to Managers)." *Managerial Planning* 27 (March-April 1979):1. **Management policy, strategy, and style, Control systems and techniques.**

A prescriptive argument for ZBB as an element of "tough-minded" management. Lots of "dos and don'ts," but no explanation of how or why.

Anthony, Robert N. "Zero-Base Budgeting: A Useful Fraud?" *Government Accountants Journal* 26 (Summer 1977):7-10. **Analytical methods, Decisionmaking, Organization and management theory.**

A look at the positive outcomes (improved financial control) that are possible with ZBB. Since the author concedes that it is impossible to install ZBB in organizations, I am not so sure the case is made. This is worth reading, however, because of its pragmatic stance.

Barton, M. Frank, Jr., and Waldron, Darryl G. "Zero-Based Budgeting: Is It New, or Unique?" *Woman CPA* 41 (January 1979):15-17. **Budgeting, Control systems and techniques.**

The authors have nothing to say.

Beckerman, Norton S. "The Missing Link: The Planning Portion of the Zero Base Approach." *Government Accountants Journal* 27 (Winter 1978-79):24-33. **Planning, Control systems and techniques.**

A formal exercise in broadening the conception of ZBB to more closely resemble the now-defunct planning-programming-budgeting (PPB) system. Hope springs eternal in the breasts of controllers.

Broadnax, Walter D. "Zero-Base Budgeting: A New Budgeting Technique, Management Tool or State of Mind?" *Government Accountants Journal* 26 (Winter 1978):26-29. **Analytical methods.**

A contradictory, confusing essay. This is one of the worst examples of attempts to understand ZBB.

Brown, Richard L. "Can Zero-Base Budgeting Be Successfully Applied to the Federal Budget Process?" *Managerial Planning* 27 (May-June 1979):9-13. **Budgeting, Evaluation.**

This article outlines the reasons why ZBB is impossible in the U.S. federal government without coming to that conclusion. The author is the Controller of the General Accounting Office (GAO) and has an obvious interest in expanding program evaluation, a key element of ZBB.

Cheek, Logan M. *Zero-Base Budgeting Comes of Age.* New York: AMACOM, 1977. **Planning, programming, and budgeting, Control systems and techniques.**

A proselytizing effort that is long on exhortation and short on empirical evidence. Cheek assumes that incremental budgeting is non-rational and not cost effective, as is ZBB. He stresses a rational, formalistic approach—as a descendant of PPB.

————. "Zero Base Budgeting in Washington." *Business Horizons* 21 (June 1978):23-28. **Planning, Management in public organizations.**

A rather shallow "appraisal" of ZBB in government. The author adds nothing to what we already know.

Cowen, Scott S. "ZBB—Where and How It Has Worked." *Business* 29 (May-June 1979):44-52. **Control systems and techniques, Budgeting.**

A good survey of ZBB use in the private and public sectors. Results are mixed, but ZBB is applied and is more successful in limited cases in industry.

————; Dean, Burton V.; and Lohrasbi, Ardeshir. "Zero Based Budgeting as a Management Tool." *MSU Business Topics* 26 (Spring 1978):29-39. **Control systems and techniques, Budgeting, Accounting.**

A naive examination of ZBB and budgeting in general. The authors choose to ignore practically all knowledge in this area.

Dean, Burton V., and Cowen, Scott S. "Zero-Base Budgeting in the Private Sector." *Business Horizons* 22 (August 1979):73-83. **Control systems and techniques, Budgeting.**

Computerized ZBB as an answer to the problems in the process. There is no explanation of how this is to be done.

Draper, Dale F., and Pitsvada, Bernard T. "Zero-Base Budgeting in the Federal Government: Some Preliminary Observations on the First Year's Effort." *Government Accountants Journal* 27 (Spring 1978):22-30. **Management in public organizations, Budgeting.**

True believers expounding on the merits of ZBB. This article is obviously intended to reinforce a formal policy of ZBB installation. There is an unquestioned acceptance of the assumptions and efficacy of the process.

Goldman, Henry H. "Priorities in Public Budgeting." *Managerial Planning* 27 (March-April 1979):25-26. **Management in public organizations, Budgeting.**

The tax revolt and ZBB—a true believer's testimony. Worthless evaluation.

Hermanson, Roger H. "A New Era of Budget Philosophy on the Federal Scene: ZBB—How to Make It Work." *Government Accountants Journal* 26 (Summer 1977):11-14. **Management in public organizations, Budgeting.**

Four pages on how to make ZBB work in one of the most complex organizational networks in the world. Ridiculous.

———, and Minmier, George S. "A Look at Zero-Base Budgeting: The Georgia Experience." *Atlanta Economic Review* 26 (July-August 1976):5-12. **Management in public organizations, Management accounting.**

Report of a survey of budget analysis in Georgia. The data show mixed responses, yet the authors come up with positive conclusions: ZBB is better than previous practices. See other Georgia studies, e.g., Lauth.

Herzlinger, Regina E. "Zero-Base Budgeting in the Federal Government: A Case Study." *Sloan Management Review* 21 (Winter 1979):3-14. **Budgeting, Control systems and techniques.**

An excellent account of the ZBB experience in the Public Health Service. Result: Formal installation but no improvement (and some impairment) of budget preparation.

Lauth, Thomas P. "Zero-Base Budgeting in Georgia State Government: Myth and Reality." *Public Administration Review* 28 (September-October 1978):420-30. **Budgeting, Management in public organizations, Control systems and techniques.**

An examination of the ZBB experience in Georgia. Not all the promised benefits have been realized, but there have been some minor process changes.

Lawrence, Floyd G. "Zero Base Budgeting: Cure or Curse?" *Industry Week* 196 (20 March 1978):94-98. **Budgeting, Control systems and techniques.**

A worthwhile review of some of the problems associated with installing ZBB in organizations.

Letzkus, William C. "Zero-Base Budgeting: Some Implications of Measuring Accomplishments." *Government Accountants Journal* 27 (Summer 1978):34-42. **Performance appraisal, Control systems and techniques.**

A formalistic discussion of ZBB as a performance appraisal instrument. There are some useful observations on competing goals, but no suggestions on how to handle the situation under systems like ZBB.

MacFarlane, John A. "Zero Base Budgeting in Action: There's Nothing to It." *CA Magazine* 109 (December 1976):28-32. **Planning, programming, and budgeting, Budgeting.**

The authors argue that there is a marked similarity between ZBB and program budgeting (PPB). This is an account of a university's experience with ZBB.

———. "Zero Base Budgeting in Action." *Accountants Digest* 43 (September 1977):28-32. **Control systems and techniques, Management accounting.**

A statement on ZBB installation at a university. Follow-up research is needed to evaluate its impact. (Nothing is added from his earlier article.)

McCandless, Henry E. "The Behavioural Side of Zero Base Budgeting: From Trust to Truth." *CA Magazine* 111 (November 1978):45. **Performance appraisal, Budgeting, Decisionmaking.**

Another look at ZBB—this time not as a tool, but as a process requiring major organizational change.

McGinnis, James F. "Plusses and Minuses of Zero-Base Budgeting." *Administrative Management* 37 (September 1976):22.

The author just discovered ZBB.

McHugh, Joseph A. "What Will Zero-Base Budgeting Mean to the Department of Defense?" *Armed Forces Comptroller* 22 (November 1977):4-7. **Management in public organizations, Control systems and techniques.**

A trite statement on ZBB. The plethora of inane articles on this subject reflects the power of buzz words.

Neumann, Bruce R. et al. "Accountants' Role in Zero-Base Budgeting." *CPA Journal* 48 (January 1978):23-27. **Accounting, Budgeting.**

A formal look at the accountants' role in ZBB.

Phare, Rowland G. "Beyond Zero-Base Budgeting." *Managerial Planning* 28 (July-August 1979):18-23. **Planning, Control systems and techniques.**

What lies beyond ZBB? Why zero-base planning, of course. ZBP seems even more remote, but it makes the alphabet soup more varied.

Phelps, William W. "Zero-Base Budgeting: Practical Implementation." *Managerial Planning* 26 (July-August 1977):35-39. **Project management, Budgeting.**

Another ZBB checklist. Not much use.

Pyhrr, Peter A. *Zero-Base Budgeting.* New York: John Wiley, 1973. **Budgeting, Control systems and techniques.**

The very popular book that started all the fuss. Whether one agrees with the feasibility of ZBB or not, this book must be read to understand what all the discussion is about. Most systems installed in organizations are adaptations or derivations from Pyhrr's formulas. **Recommended.**

————. "Zero-Base Budgeting: Where to Use It and How to Begin." *SAM Advanced Management Journal* 41 (Summer 1976):4-14. **Budgeting, Control systems and techniques.**

A short exhortation from the popularizer of ZBB. This article presents nothing new, little that is worthwhile, and can safely be ignored.

————. "The Zero-Base Approach to Government Budgeting." *Public Administration Review* 37 (January-February 1977):1-8. **Budgeting, Control systems and techniques.**

Peter Pyhrr rides again. ZBB explained (again).

Reckers, Philip M. J. "Zero Base Budgeting: A New Home in the Federal Government?" *Goverment Accountants Journal* 26 (Spring 1977):40-46. **Management in public organizations, Control systems and techniques.**

The authors argue that the key to successful implementation of ZBB is proper organizational preparation. How?

————, and Stagliano, A. J. "Zero-Base Budgeting." *Management Accounting* 59 (November 1977):18-20. **Budgeting.**

Another formal, too-short explanation of ZBB that is not much help to anyone.

Rehfuss, John. "Zero-Base Budgeting: The Experience to Date." *Public Personnel Management* 6 (May-June 1977):181-87. **Planning, programming, and budgeting, Management in public organizations.**

An early tentative survey of the ZBB experience in city and state government. The author makes a point of distinguishing ZBB from program budgeting, whereas more recent accounts move the two closer.

Scheiring, Michael J. "Zero-Base Budgeting in New Jersey." *State Government* 49 (Summer 1976):174-79. **Management in public organizations, Budgeting.**

A ritual look at ZBB in state government. The author is a believer, so there is little to be learned from this.

Schick, Allen. "The Road from ZBB." *Public Administration Review* 38 (March-April 1978):177-80. **Budgeting, Management in public organizations.**

A short update on status of ZBB reforms in the U.S. federal government, as of the 1979 budget.

Suver, James D., and Brown, Ray L. "Where Does Zero-Based Budgeting Work?" *Harvard Business Review* 55 (November-December 1977):76-84. **Budgeting.**

A pro-con discussion of ZBB that comes down on the pro side. But some interesting misunderstandings are brought out along the way.

Watkins, William, Jr. "Evaluating Zero Based Budgeting." *Managerial Planning* 27 (September-October 1978):34-37. **Budgeting, Organizational behavior.**

More ZBB—nothing new. It needs top management backing, etc.

Analytical Methods and Quantitative Techniques

ANALYTICAL METHODS

Brewer, Garry D. "What's the Purpose? What's the Use? A Review of a *Management Science* Special Issue on 'Urban Issues II'." *Interfaces* 4 (February 1974):60-74. **Evaluation and program effectiveness, Management in public organizations.**

An intelligent review that stands as an original essay on reviewing and management science techniques by one of the more pragmatic people in the field.

Burton, Gene E., and Pathak, Dev. S. "Social Character and Group Decision Making." *SAM Advanced Management Journal* 43 (Summer 1978):12-20. **Decisionmaking, Decision models.**

A study of the relative merits of nominal groups (NGT) and interacting groups in generating ideas and reaching acceptable group decisions. An interesting appraisal of some popular group techniques.

Gordon, Paul J. "Fantastic Medication: Wrong Disease!" *Scientific and Behavioral Foundations for Decision Analysis,* edited by L. J. Moore and S. M. Lee. Atlanta: Southeast Region of the American Institute for Decision Sciences, 1974, pp. 192-93. **Management education and training, Problem solving.**

A fascinating essay on material that is presented as useful, but may prove to be worse than useless. This subject deserves better and more extensive treatment than the author provides here.

Gorman, Ronald H., and Baker, H. Kent. "Brainstorming Your Way to Problem-Solving Ideas." *Personnel Journal* 57 (August 1978):438-56. **Problem solving.**

A formal outline of brainstorming as a problem-solving technique.

Jacobs, Richard A. "Project Management: A New Style for Success." *SAM Advanced Management Journal* 41 (Autumn 1976):4-14. **Project management, Organizational growth and change, Organizational learning.**

A sketchy outline on how to handle one-time "project situations." It is hard to understand what the author is talking about. There are a lot of jargon and buzz words and little content.

Ladd, George W. "Artistic Research Tools for Scientific Minds." *American Journal of Agricultural Economics* 61 (February 1979):1-11. **Problem solving, Management education and training.**

An excellent essay on the use and non-use of the various techniques invented to aid or inform inquiry but which may in fact inhibit it. Intelligent and well-written, this piece is not only for the scientist or academic.

Lewis, C. D. "Change Identification: A Necessary Prerequisite for Management by Exception." *Management Decision* 14 (1976):129-47. **Control systems and techniques, Organizational learning.**

A technical exercise in identifying change or "deviation from plan." This article is hard to follow and is very likely difficult to use.

Michael, George C. "A Review of Heuristic Programming." *Decision Sciences* 3 (1972):74-100. **Problem solving.**

This is not for the casual reader. It is a detailed examination of the potential for heuristic *programs* in handling ill-structured problems.

Pavitt, Keith. "Analytical Techniques in Government Science Policy." *Futures* 4 (March 1972):5-12. **Technology transfer, Public policy.**

An interesting review of several analytic techniques and their potential use or misuse in developing policy.

Rivlin, Alice M. *Systematic Thinking for Social Action.* Washington, D.C.: Brookings Institution, 1971. **Systems analysis, Policy analysis.**

An intelligent discussion of the various approaches to "systematic thinking" in designing and evaluating federal social action programs. You do not have to agree with Rivlin to appreciate her keen analysis; but the emphasis on comprehensiveness in design and implementation can be sensibly questioned.

Sneddon, L. M. "Decision Analysis for Top Management." *Long Range Planning* 3 (September 1970):50-56. **Decision analysis, Management accounting.**

A few simple analytic financial tools presented as magic decisionmaking aids. This article is full of *implicit* questionable assumptions and subjective probabilities.

Tanur, Judith M. et al., eds. *Statistics: A Guide to the Unknown.* San Francisco: Holden-Day, 1972. **Modeling and simulation, Decision models.**

A reasonably good effort at explaining the use and misuse of statistical analysis. Some technical familiarity is assumed, but the book is generally useful.

Young, Michael S. "FMRR: A Clever Hoax?" *Appraisal Journal* 47 (July 1979):359-69. **Management accounting, Decision theory.**

A critique of internal rate of return (IRR) and refinements (FMRR) as financial decision rules. The author proposes the tried and true net present value (NPV) as a more useful technique.

COST-BENEFIT ANALYSIS

Bogar, Carl F. "Problems in Estimating Costs for Acquiring New Weapons." *GAO Review* 6 (Winter 1971):61-65. **Budgeting, Auditing, Planning.**

A short essay on GAO's experience in cost estimates for new weapons systems. Forcing early prediction can be counter-productive in that estimates are deliberately set low, thereby producing gigantic cost-overruns.

Trinkl, Frank H. "Allocations Among Programs Having Counteractive Outcomes." *Policy Sciences* 3 (July 1972):163-76. **Policy analysis, Modeling and simulation.**

A technical mathematical modeling effort that is only for those very interested in such exercises.

ECONOMIC ANALYSIS

Armstrong, J. Scott. "Forecasting with Econometric Methods: Folklore versus Fact." *Journal of Business* 51 (October 1978):549-64. **Analytical methods, Planning.**

A comparison of the belief in econometric forecasts and the evidence for forecasting accuracy. Empirically, econometrics has not been very accurate, yet economists avoid the evidence and retain the belief. **Recommended.**

Arrow, Kenneth J. "Limited Knowledge and Economic Analysis." *American Economic Review* 64 (March 1974):1-10. **Risk and uncertainty.**

An American Economic Association (AEA) presidential address, reflecting Arrow's concern with "ignorance of the economic agent." Of limited interest.

Chow, Gregory C. "Are Econometric Methods Useful for Forecasting?" *Journal of Business* 51 (October 1978):565-68. **Analytical methods, Planning.**

A critique of Armstrong's study of econometrics in forecasting. The author will not change his belief in econometrics on the basis of the evidence presented. Would he ever?

OPERATIONS RESEARCH AND MANAGEMENT SCIENCE

Ackoff, Russell L. "Science in the Systems Age: Beyond IE, OR, and MS." *Operations Research* 21 (May-June 1973):661-71. **Systems theory, Organization and management theory.**

An excellent example of the overblown verbiage of "systems" writing. There are some good statements regarding analysis (decomposition) and synthesis (design).

――――. "The Future of Operational Research Is Past." *Journal of the Operational Research Society* 30 (1979):93-104. **Organization and management theory.**

A good discussion of OR practice and theory and the relationship to real organizations. A wide-ranging statement addressing particular organizational and managerial concerns.

――――. "Resurrecting the Future of Operational Research." *Journal of the Operational Research Society* 30 (1979):189-99. **Organization and management theory.**

Not as good as "Future of OR Is Past," because Ackoff provides an academic solution to real problems raised in "Future." Ackoff argues that utility of OR must be demonstrated, but he does not explain "Why OR?" He also proposes a new approach to organizational analysis: S^3 (social systems sciences).

Anderson, John C., and Hoffmann, Thomas R. "A Perspective on the Implementation of Management Science." *Academy of Management Review* 3 (July 1978):563-71. **Organizational effectiveness.**

This is a mediocre exercise letting us know how to implement OR/MS in organizations. The authors offer a "conceptual framework" that does not tell us how to do it.

Barth, Richard T., and Vertinsky, Ilan. "Organizational Form and OR/MS Implementation in Colombia." *Quarterly Journal of Management Development* 4 (June 1973):1-12. **Organizational design, Decisionmaking.**

A study of OR/MS application and organizational form in Colombia. This is an interesting study in that the authors conclude that existing organizational patterns must be changed to successfully install more formal OR/MS techniques.

Beall, R. B. "The Influence of Measurement in the Development of Management Science." *Omega* 2 (1974):593-605. **Systems approach, Analytical methods.**

A quick once-over on the effect of quantification on management approaches. The author's purpose is not clear. Lots of "systems" verbiage.

Beer, Stafford. *Decision and Control.* New York: John Wiley, 1966. **Organization and management theory, Control systems and techniques.**

An update on operations research and management cybernetics. This is not an easy book to get through, but it is worth the effort. Formal mathematics, logic, philosophy, and pragmatic concerns are mixed and addressed, with varying degrees of success.

Bevan, R. G. "Operational Research and the Pluralist Frame of Reference." *Omega* 3 (1975):699-708. **Organizational communication, Cost-benefit analysis.**

A sensible article—one of the few to discuss conflict in any detail. The author uses some of T. C. Schelling's work to illustrate communication problems and their role in reaching "satisficing" solutions. There is a good, short criticism of cost-benefit analysis.

Blackett, P. M. S. "Operational Research." *Advancement of Science* 5 (April 1948):26-37. **Research and development, Management history.**

It's old but it's good. If you want to know how operations research began and how far it is from its origins, read this. (Also see Crowther and Whiddington, *Science at War;* Jones, *The Wizard War;* and Morse and Kimball, *Methods of Operations Research.*) **Recommended.**

Bonder, Seth. "Operations Research Education: Some Requirements and Deficiencies." *Operations Research* 21 (May-June 1973):796-809. **Control systems and techniques, Management education and training.**

A critique of the solution-orientation in OR education. There are some interesting comments on modeling and error correction.

————. "Changing the Future of Operations Research." *Operations Research* 27 (March-April 1979):209-24.

An examination of the immediate past and potential future of operations research as a distinct professional discipline.

Caywood, Thomas E. "How Can We Improve Operations Research?" *Operations Research* 18 (July-August 1970):569-72. **Control systems and techniques.**

A retiring ORSA presidential address. Caywood's concerns are still timely.

Churchman, C. West; Ackoff, Russell L.; and Arnoff, E. Leonard. *Introduction to Operations Research*. New York: John Wiley, 1957. **Control systems and techniques, Analytical methods.**

A good, sensible, early introductory OR text; as good a primer as is likely to be found. The advances in OR since 1957 are technological and do not necessarily affect the sense of this book.

————, and Schainblatt, A. H. "The Researcher and the Manager: A Dialectic of Implementation." *Management Science* 11 (February 1965): B69-87. **Policy analysis, Manager and controller roles.**

An academic discussion of the difficulties in meshing the concerns of researchers and managers. Little has changed since this was written.

Crowther, J. G., and Whiddington, R. *Science at War*. New York: Philosophical Library, 1948. **Management history.**

A fascinating account of how operations research started in Britain in the early days of World War II. Long out of print, but worth looking for. Also see Jones, *The Wizard War*.

Czepiel, John A., and Hertz, Paul. "Management Science in Major Merchandising Firms." *Journal of Retailing* 52 (Winter 1975-76):3. **Control systems and techniques.**

An interesting study that reveals a low rate of OR/MS use in major retail firms. The authors discuss reasons for low acceptance, but they do not question management science techniques' efficacy in merchandising.

Drucker, Peter F. "The Performance Gap in Management Science: Reasons and Remedies." *Organizational Dynamics* 2 (Autumn 1973):19-29. **Control systems and techniques, Organization and management theory.**

A sensible statement. Although it contains nothing new, it does emphasize uncertainty and decision without involved mathematical formulations.

Ebert, Ronald J. "Environmental Structure and Programmed Decision Effectiveness." *Management Science* 19 (December 1972):435-45. **Decision analysis, Decision models.**

Decisionmaking in closed-set programmable circumstances, a condition that does not obtain in most managerial tasks.

Edie, Leslie C. "The Quality and Maturity of OR." *Operations Research* 21 (September-October 1973):1024-29. **Systems analysis, Organization and management theory.**

Another retirement address by a past president of the Operations Research Society of America (ORSA), reflecting the confusion and searching that is still with us.

Fenske, Russell W. "A Taxonomy for Operations Research." *Operations Research* 19 (January-February 1971):224-34.

A classification scheme developed for ORSA that might be useful for researchers and OR professionals.

Fitzgerald, Paddy. "The Role and Needs of the Management Science Practitioner." *Omega* 6 (1978):231-36. **Consultants, Analytical methods.**

A British view of management science that is much more pragmatic than American preachings. This is a good sensible piece; the author is not taken in by the mythical status of management science in the U.S.

Fries, Brant E. "Bibliography of Operations Research in Health-Care Systems." *Operations Research* 24 (September-October 1976):801-14. **Policy analysis.**

An excellent bibliography with a narrow focus, this is a good shortcut for those interested in *applied* OR.

Fuller, Jack A., and Atherton, Roger M. "Fitting in the Management Science Specialist." *Business Horizons* 22 (April 1979):14-17. **Analytical methods, Control systems and techniques.**

A short, but useful discussion of the problems between managers and management science specialists. The author says that the benefits businesses get from quantitative tools and techniques are "immeasurable." Curious!

Gaither, Norman. "The Adoption of Operations Research Techniques by Manufacturing Organizations." *Decision Sciences* 6 (October 1975): 797-813. **Control systems and techniques.**

A carefully crafted study of OR adoptions. Not surprisingly, OR use is more prevalent in firms engaged in well-known technological domains in relatively certain activities.

Grayson, C. Jackson, Jr. "Management Science and Business Practice." *Harvard Business Review* 51 (July-August 1973):41-48. **Organizational effectiveness, Organizational control.**

One of the most intelligent and telling critiques of management science, this article has become a classic. **Highly recommended.**

Gruber, William H., and Niles, John S. "Problems in the Utilization of Management Science/Operations Research: A State of the Art Survey." *Interfaces* 2 (1971):12-19. **Organization and management theory.**

A sensible statement. Short and succinct.

Hammond, John S. "The Roles of the Manager and Management Scientist in Successful Implementation." *Sloan Management Review* 15 (Winter 1974):1-24. **Manager and controller roles, Decision analysis.**

A summary of OR/MS clichés. Nothing new or useful.

Hertz, David B. "Does Management Science Influence Management Action?" *Columbia Journal of World Business* 12 (Fall 1977):105-12. **Management information systems, Managerial functions.**

A wordy piece with little substance, by a management consultant. His terms and concepts are confused. Avoid, except as an example of ascendant cliché.

Jewell, William S. "Operations Research in the Insurance Industry: Part 1, A Survey of Applications." *Operations Research* 22 (September-October 1974):918-28. **Risk and uncertainty, Control systems and techniques.**

A sensible discussion of operations research in an appropriate industry. Probably only of interest to OR professionals and insurance managers.

Klein, Dieter, and Butkovich, Paul. "Can the Professions of Operations Research/Management Science Change and Survive?" *Interfaces* 6 (May 1976):47-51. **Organizational growth and change, Control systems and techniques.**

An insightful critique of the OR/MS myth and the potential for change. The authors are not optimistic, given the self-reinforcing system (mostly academic) that the profession has become.

Levitt, Theodore. "A Heretical View of Management 'Science'." *Fortune* 98 (18 December 1978):50-52. **Organization and management theory, Analytical methods.**

A biting critique of the various techniques that make things more obscure than necessary.

McCloskey, Joseph F.; Trefethen, Florence N.; and Coppinger, John M., eds. *Operations Research for Management.* 2 vols. Baltimore: The Johns Hopkins University Press, 1954. **Management history, Control systems and techniques.**

A classic set, this is the definitive collection of essays on the American view of operations research through the fifties.

Mjosund, Arne. "The Synergy of Operations Research and Computers." *Operations Research* 20 (September-October 1972):1057-64. **Computer services, Organization and management theory.**

One of the better statements on the lack of interaction between OR specialists and computer systems designers. Mjosund comments on the OR shift from problem to method.

Morse, Philip M., ed. *Operations Research for Public Systems.* Cambridge, Mass.: The MIT Press, 1967. **Control systems and techniques, Management in public organizations.**

A formal outline of operations research. The appropriate use of OR in public agencies, beyond scheduling and routing, is still questionable.

————, and Kimball, George E. *Methods of Operations Research.* Rev. ed. New York: John Wiley, 1951. **Management history, Control systems and techniques.**

Primarily of historical interest, this book is in many ways the American equivalent of Crowther and Whiddington's *Science at War.*

Neal, Rodney D., and Radnor, Michael. "The Relation Between Formal Procedures for Pursuing OR/MS Activities and OR/MS Group Success." *Operations Research* 21 (March-April 1973):451-74. **Control systems and techniques.**

A useful look at various definitions of OR/MS successes. The authors point out the lack of research in this area.

Noble, Carl, and Thornhill, Virgil. "Institutionalization of Management Science in the Multinational Firm." *Columbia Journal of World Business* 12 (Fall 1977):9-22. **Comparative management, Organizational design.**

A prescriptive and formalistic article on how to succeed in multinational business with management science.

Radnor, Michael. "Management Sciences and Policy Sciences." *Policy Sciences* 2 (December 1971):447-56. **Policy analysis, Systems analysis.**

A critique of policy science as an extension of the exaggerated claims of management science. Some vacuous claims for systems analysis.

————, and Neal, Rodney D. "The Progress of Management-Science Activities in Large US Industrial Corporations." *Operations Research* 21 (March-April 1973):427-50. **Control systems and techniques, Analytical methods.**

A good empirical examination of OR/MS application and professional direction in the U.S. This is worthwhile even though it has some questionable assumptions and conclusions.

————; Rubenstein, Albert H.; and Tansik, David A. "Implementation in Operations Research and R&D in Government and Business Organizations." *Operations Research* 18 (November-December 1970):967-91. **Research and development, Organizational effectiveness.**

An indication of the growing concern with implementation and operations research in the late sixties.

Rubenstein, Albert H. et al. "Some Organizational Factors Related to the Effectiveness of Management Science Groups in Industry." *Management Science* 13 (April 1967):B508-18. **Organizational design, Control systems and techniques.**

The authors offer some suggestions on installing effective OR/MS groups. Based on a manufacturing firm case study, the key is management use of OR/MS recommendations.

Shuchman, Abe. *Scientific Decision Making in Business: Readings in Operations Research for Nonmathematicians.* New York: Holt, Rinehart, and Winston, 1963. **Analytical methods, Control systems and techniques.**

An old text that provides a somewhat painless introduction to operations research. This is not simple, but the non-mathematician will have an easier time with this book than with most OR texts.

Smith, R. D., and Robey, D. "Research and Applications in Operations Management: Discussion of a Paradox." *Academy of Management Journal* 16 (December 1973):647-57. **Control systems and techniques, Organization and management theory.**

A review of the promise and misconceptions of production control systems. The authors seek a better understanding of real-world constraints that limit system utility.

Spindler, Arthur. "Social and Rehabilitation Services: A Challenge to Operations Research." *Operations Research* 18 (November-December 1970):1112-24. **Policy analysis.**

A narrow interpretation of operations research applications in social programs. The methodological emphasis ignores the benefits of program duplication and overlap.

Tomlinson, Rolfe C. "OR, Organizational Design and Adaptivity." *Omega* 4 (1976):527-37. **Organizational design, Decision models.**

An intelligent assessment of OR in changing organizational circumstances. **Recommended**.

Turban, Efraim. "A Sample Survey of Operations Research Activities at the Corporate Level." *Operations Research* 20 (May-June 1972):708-21. **Management policy, strategy, and style.**

A survey of OR practice marked by faulty research design and analysis. Survey respondents claim (1) high turnover rates for OR people, (2) the simplest methods are used the most, and (3) a high rate of OR implementation. One hundred seven OR directors responded to 475 *mailed* questionnaires.

Wagle, B. "Management Science and Strategic Planning." *Long Range Planning* 4 (April 1971):26-33. **Planning, Modeling and simulation.**

An example of context-free recommendations and a failure to learn from experiences with strategic planning.

Wagner, Harvey M. "The ABC's of OR." *Operations Research* 19 (1979): 1259-81. **Control systems and techniques, Management models.**

A good review of OR/MS and the move away from practical operating problems.

White, Michael J. *Management Science in Federal Agencies: The Adoption and Diffusion of a Socio-Technical Innovation.* Lexington, Mass.: D.C. Heath, 1975. **Analytical methods, Management in public organizations.**

A survey of MS applications in federal departments. It is hard to see how some of the techniques can be considered "innovations" in the positive sense implied by the author.

————; Radnor, Michael; and Tansik, David A., eds. *Management and Policy Science in American Government.* Lexington, Mass.: D.C. Heath, 1975. **Policy analysis, Evaluation and project effectiveness, Management in public organizations.**

This is a reasonable collection of articles. The editors provide integrating essays and have divided the book into sections that permit ready reference. **Recommended.**

Woolsey, Robert E. D., and Swanson, Huntington S. *Operations Research for Immediate Application.* New York: Harper and Row, 1975. **Analytical methods, Problem solving.**

A glorious *tour de force*. Woolsey is a master at de-mystifying OR and making it *operational* in the original sense. This book is straightforward and deceptively simple. Could have been titled OR for non-believers. **Recommended.**

PERT AND CPM

Grasberg, Eugene. "Development Project Format: A Design for Maximum Information." *Ekistics* 26 (August 1968):162-72. **Project management, Management in developing countries.**

A how and why-to-do-it description of PERT applied to development project management. The author gives a clear explanation, but he does not question the technique's efficacy in uncertain domains. Useful, but misleading.

Johnson, James R. "Advance Project Control." *Journal of Systems Management* 28 (May 1977):24-27. **Control systems and techniques, Project management.**

Another PERT rule book: Ten steps to control *any* project (that's what the man said).

Krakowski, Martin. "PERT and Parkinson's Law." *Interfaces* 5 (November 1974):35-40. **Organizational effectiveness, Control systems and techniques.**

Witty, intelligent, and devastating. Krakowski gives us no heavy theorizing or data, just barbed comment.

Krogstad, Jack L.; Grudnitski, Gary; and Bryant, David W. "PERT and PERT/Cost for Audit Planning and Control." *Journal of Accountancy* 144 (November 1977):82-91. **Evaluation, Auditing.**

Should be read in context after Krakowski's "PERT and Parkinson's Law." Note that this appeared exactly three years later.

Ryan, William G. "Management Practice and Research—Poles Apart." *Business Horizons* 20 (June 1977):23-29. **Analytical methods, Organization and management theory.**

An examination of the distinction between academic research premises and management practices. This is a worthwhile piece that is short and to the point.

Sauls, Eugene. "The Use of GERT." *Journal of Systems Management* 23 (August 1972):18-22. **Control systems and techniques.**

A problem. The author outlines a PERT derivative that broadens the scope of application at the cost of increased complexity, which may reduce the scope.

Swanson, Lloyd A., and Pazer, Harold L. "Implications of the Underlying Assumptions of PERT." *Decision Sciences* 2 (October 1971):461-80. **Control systems and techniques.**

A mathematical exercise demonstrating basic errors in PERT calculations. The conclusions must be read since the author points out a lack of empirical evidence for PERT's utility.

SYSTEMS ANALYSIS

Ackoff, Russell L. "The Systems Revolution." *Long Range Planning* 7 (December 1974):2-20. **Planning, Organization and management theory.**

A rather verbose, occasionally obscure exposition on systems, organizations, and management and control.

Archibald, K.A. "Three Views of the Expert's Role in Policymaking: Systems Analysis, Incrementalism, and the Clinical Approach." *Policy Sciences* 1 (1970):73-86. **Incrementalism, Policymaking.**

A good summary of systems analysis and the incremental approach. The clinical synthesis is jumbled, but it is worth a look.

Bell, David; Keeney, Ralph L.; and Raiffa, Howard, eds. *Conflicting Objectives in Decisions.* New York: John Wiley, 1977. **Decision analysis, Analytical methods.**

An uneven, technical collection of essays on "applied systems analysis." Questions arise as to who is to apply systems analysis and how.

Berlinski, David. *On Systems Analysis.* Cambridge, Mass.: The MIT Press. 1976. **Systems theory, Control systems and techniques.**

Brilliant negativism. This is probably the best critique of systems analysis, general systems theory, and cybernetics. Berlinski devastates not only the assumptions of systems approaches, but their simplistic mathematical underpinnings as well. **Highly recommended.**

Black, Guy. *The Application of Systems Analysis to Government Operations.* New York: Praeger, 1968. **Management in public organizations, Policy analysis.**

A formalistic approach to applied systems analysis in government, this is one of similar works that do little to improve our understanding of government or systems analysis.

Brewer, Garry D. *Systems Analysis in the Urban Complex: Potential and Limitations.* P-5141. Santa Monica, Calif.: RAND Corporation, December 1973. **Policy analysis, Problem solving.**

An excellent (though quite academic) survey of systems analysis and its applications. **Recommended.**

Emery, F. E., ed. *Systems Thinking: Selected Readings.* Baltimore: Penguin Books, 1969. **Systems approach, Systems theory.**

An excellent collection that contains representative essays from many luminaries in systems thinking and some useful integrating articles. **Recommended.**

Hitch, Charles J. *Decision-Making for Defense.* Berkeley: University of California Press, 1965. **Management history, Decisionmaking.**

Though really a product of the fifties, Hitch's influence on approaches to organizations, society, and problem solving dictates a need for familiarity with his work.

————, and McKean, Roland N. *The Economics of Defense in the Nuclear Age.* Cambridge, Mass.: Harvard University Press, 1961. **Management history, Decisionmaking.**

Probably the best single source of the ideas that have informed U.S. governmental programs since the fifties. The concern with "effective-efficient" management in government found comprehensive expression in the work of Hitch, McKean, and the RAND cohort (including James Schlesinger).

Hoos, Ida R. "Can Systems Analysis Solve Social Problems?" *Datamation* 20 (June 1974):82-92. **Systems approach, Control systems and techniques.**

Hoos, a brilliant social scientist and polemicist, is at her best here. **Recommended.**

Hopeman, Richard J. *Systems Analysis and Operations Management.* Columbus, Ohio: Charles E. Merrill, 1969. **Operations research and management science, Control systems and techniques.**

A typically formal outline of systems analysis applications. We tend to forget how temporally contextual analytic approaches tend to be; this is a good reminder.

McKean, Roland N. *Efficiency in Government Through Systems Analysis, With Emphasis on Water Resources Development.* New York: John Wiley, 1958. **Analytical methods, Management history.**

An early statement on systems analysis in government. Water resource control is where cost-benefit analysis got started.

————, ed. *Issues in Defense Economics.* New York: National Bureau of Economic Research, 1967. **Analytical methods, Management history.**

Another classic in the early applications of systems analysis in defense planning.

Optner, Stanford L., ed. *Systems Analysis.* Baltimore: Penguin, 1973. **Systems theory, Organization and management theory.**

Selected readings from the fifties to the seventies. A good collection, though somewhat incomplete because of size limitations.

Quade, E. S. *Analysis for Public Decisions.* New York: American Elsevier, 1975. **Policy analysis, Decision analysis.**

Quade extends his earlier work in military/defense applications into general public policy. The leap is not as grand as may first appear. Systems analysis is not limited to specific issues.

————, and Boucher, W. I., eds. *Systems Analysis and Policy Planning: Applications in Defense.* New York: American Elsevier, 1968. **Policy analysis.**

Some of the essays in this collection are too technically oriented to be of much general use, but Quade's chapters on systems analysis are worth looking at. Also see James Schlesinger's essay.

Rudwick, Bernard H. *Systems Analysis for Effective Planning: Principles and Cases.* New York: John Wiley, 1969. **Planning, Systems theory.**

A cookbook of systems analysis principles. Nothing is added to the knowledge of systems. This is simply an example of the comprehensive optimism of the sixties.

Schlesinger, James R. *Systems Analysis and the Political Process.* P-3464. Santa Monica, Calif.: RAND Corporation, June 1967. **Policy analysis, Systems theory.**

An example of what this Schlesinger was doing at RAND.

Shell, Richard L., and Stelzer, David F. "Systems Analysis: Aid to Decision Making." *Business Horizons* 14 (December 1971):67-72. **Systems approach, Decisionmaking.**

The usual "systems analysis does everything" argument. Skip it unless you need an example of systems analysis dogma.

Stinchcombe, Arthur L. "Communications." *American Political Science Review* 68 (September 1974):1262-64. **Policy analysis, Organization and management theory.**

A sensible guide to the potential for charlatanry in "systems analysis." **Highly recommended.**

Szanton, Peter L. "Systems Problems in the City." *Operations Research* 20 (May-June 1972):765-73. **Policy analysis, Evaluation.**

A sensible statement on the politics of evaluation and error-correction. This is an interesting discussion of ambiguous or hidden goals, with two illustrative case studies.

SYSTEMS APPROACH

Byron, Robert J. "The Systems Approach to Operational Development in Municipalities." *Journal of Systems Management* 21 (July 1970):16-26. **Management in public organizations, Policy analysis.**

An exposition on something called a "municipal information system" by an aerospace convert to city administration. I wonder what happened to the system.

Chadwick, George F. *A Systems View of Planning: Towards a Theory of the Urban and Regional Planning Process.* New York: Pergamon Press, 1971. **Policy analysis, Planning.**

Another "systems view" treatise. Chadwick's approach is typical of the attitudes of the sixties, when systems analysis was the answer to everything.

Churchman, C. West. *The Systems Approach*. New York: Dell, 1968. **Systems analysis, Organization and management theory.**

The most lucid explanation of systems analysis available. Churchman explores the limitations as well as the advantages of the "systems approach." **Recommended.**

Cooper, W. W. et al. "Systems Approaches to Urban Planning: Mixed, Conditional, Adaptive and Other Alternatives." *Policy Sciences* 2 (1971): 397-405. **Management in public organizations, Planning.**

A typical "boil-the-ocean" prescription with a lot of systems verbiage that never reveals how to deliver on the authors' claims. This is one to avoid, unless a negative example piques curiosity.

Delp, Peter, et al. *Systems Tools for Project Planning*. Bloomington: PASITAM Indiana University, 1977. **Analytical methods.**

A useful "toolkit" of various systems analytic techniques and management science gimmicks. Delp has provided a sensible outline and mapping of the techniques' uses and limitations. **Recommended.**

Johnson, Kenton H. "A Systems Approach to Solving Complex Problems." *Management Notes* 20 (January 1976):13-21. **Analytical methods, Organizational learning, Organizational goals and objectives.**

Another "how to" do everything with something called "Goal Fabric Analysis."

Kast, Fremont E., and Rosenzweig, James E. "General Systems Theory: Applications for Organization and Management." *Academy of Management Journal* 15 (December 1972):447-65. **Systems theory, Organization and management theory.**

An excellent survey of GST and the contingency views in organization and management theory. **Recommended.**

LaPatra, Jack W. *Applying the Systems Approach to Urban Development*. Stroudsburg, Pa.: Dowden, Hutchinson, and Ross, 1973. **Policy analysis, Planning.**

An attempt to apply a holistic systems approach to the problems of urban development. If this seems appealing, also see Garry Brewer's *Politicians, Bureaucrats and the Consultant*.

Mantell, Leroy H. "On the Use of Cybernetics in Management." *Management International Review* 13 (1973):33-41. **Planning, Control systems and techniques.**

A vapid, trite, and tautological exercise on systems, planning, and control.

SYSTEMS THEORY

Lucas, Henry C., Jr. *Toward Creative Systems Design.* New York: Columbia University Press, 1974. **Systems analysis, Organizational design.**

An interesting book with somewhat limited appeal because of the obscurity of the subject. Creating a "creative system" may be somewhat remote from most organizational concerns.

Millar, Jean A. "Selective Adaptation." *Policy Sciences* 3 (1972):125-35. **Computer services, Organizational effectiveness.**

A critique of cybernetics, computers, and "systems" in organizations. This is not bad, but it could be said better.

Thayer, Frederick. "General System(s) Theory: The Promise That Could Not Be Kept." *Academy of Management Journal* 15 (December 1972): 481-93. **Organization and management theory, Hierarchy.**

A rather ill-tempered critique of GST, this is an overstated and simplistic broadside that wanders all over the intellectual landscape.

Toronto, Robert S. "A General Systems Model for the Analysis of Organizational Change." *Behavioral Science* 20 (July 1975):145-56. **Organizational growth and change, Modeling and simulation.**

Super-systems strike again. This is a vague, hard-to-follow article that glosses over the general incomprehensibility of the model.

von Bertalanffry, Ludwig. *General Systems Theory: Foundations, Development, Applications.* Rev. ed. New York: George Braziller, 1968. **Systems analysis, Organization and management theory.**

General systems theory (GST) is intended as a unified explanation of everything. This is a very complex book, and its mathematical content has been criticized by Berlinski in *On Systems Analysis*; but GST has profoundly influenced many people, and this book deserves attention on that ground alone.

Computers and Information

COMPUTER SERVICES

Bernstein, Jeremy. *The Analytical Engine*. New York: Random House, 1964. **Information processing, Management history.**

A marvelous book that recounts the history of computer development from the earliest efforts at manual calculation to the modern electronic wonders. Lucid, entertaining, and informative. **Recommended.**

Burck, Gilbert. "Management Will Never Be the Same Again." *Fortune* 70 (August 1964):125. **Organizational design, Management information systems.**

This is interesting primarily because of the forecasts and predictions made. The promise of 1964 has not always been realized.

Fahey, Robert J. et al. *Computer Science and Management Dynamics*. New York: Financial Executives Research Foundation, 1969. **Control systems and techniques, Management models.**

This book is an example of those publications that advocate the total computerized organizational control system. All elements—marketing, production, and inventory—were to be linked in one grand design.

Foy, Nancy. "Computer Gloom." *European Business*, no. 37 (Spring 1973), pp. 77-79. **Organizational effectiveness, Evaluation.**

This is dated, but it is an interesting report on the real costs of computer systems in industry.

Head, Robert V. "Systems Organization and the Technology of the Future." *Journal of Systems Management* 30 (August 1979):6-11. **Control systems and techniques, Management control.**

Formalistic clichés with little substance.

Hyler, Fletcher H., and Bertocchi, Alfred M. "Coping with Computers in a Changing Environment." *Financial Executive* 47 (February 1979): 28-36. **Organizational growth and change, Decisionmaking.**

A formal argument for distributive data processing (DDP) as the answer to problems in organizational computer services.

Kintisch, Ronald S., and Weisbord, Marvin R. "Getting Computer People and Users to Understand Each Other." *SAM Advanced Management Journal* 42 (Spring 1977):4-14. **Management effectiveness.**

A useless listing of what should and should not be done.

Kraemer, Kenneth L.; Pearson, Sigfrid; Danziger, James N.; and Dutton, William H. "Chief Executives, Local Government, and Computers." *Nation's Cities* 13 (October 1975):17-40. **Electronic data processing, Management in public organizations.**

A real "gee whiz" job on how computers magically solve all the problems of local government. To be read with a handful of salt.

Martin, Keith R. "The Financial Executive and the Computer: The Continuing Struggle." *Financial Executive* 45 (March 1977):26-32. **Managerial functions, Management accounting.**

Another formal statement about what is needed in a computer-centered management and accounting system. A shopping list, and no more.

Owen, Kenneth. "The Big User's Dilemma." *Management Today* (March 1977), p. 35. **Organizational effectiveness, Control systems and techniques.**

All is not well in the computer world; the user is being left out in the quest for bigger, better, faster technology.

Steely, John E., Jr. "When Management Is Automated." *Datamation* 24 (April 1978):172-76. **Organizational growth and change, Management information systems.**

A perfect foil for those who see the computer as "taking over" society. Pure and patent nonsense, this article is good for a laugh, provided you don't believe the author's contention that we will all be obeying computer rules some day.

Tolliver, Edward M. "Myths of Automated Management Systems." *Journal of Systems Management* 22 (March 1971):29-32. **Control systems and techniques.**

A light but telling critique of computer use in organization management.

Uttal, Bro. "How the 4300 Fits I.B.M.'s New Strategy." *Fortune* 100 (30 July 1979):58-63. **Innovation.**

An update on IBM's new product line and the effect on industry and computer applications.

Vyssotsky, Victor A. "Computer Systems in Business: More Evolution than Revolution." *Management Review* 68 (February 1979):15-22. **Organizational growth and change, Decisionmaking.**

A good assessment of the once and future use of computer services in large organizations. An intelligent, balanced, and pragmatic appraisal.

Winer, Leon. "Solving the Computers-in-Marketing Problem: A Case History." *Journal of Business Research* 2 (January 1974):39-46. **Management effectiveness, Management policy, strategy, and style.**

An account of how short seminars can be used to improve marketing managers' understanding of computers. There was no follow-up to see if this produced increased *use*.

Worthley, John A., and Heaphey, James J. "Computer Technology and Public Administration in State Government." *Bureaucrat* 7 (Fall 1978): 32-37. **Control systems and techniques, Management in public organizations.**

An unconvincing and inconsistently presented argument for a "new perspective" on computer usage. The authors would design organizations to fit computer technology, i.e., a centralized EDP facility serving all elements.

DATA BASES

Romney, Marshall B. "Should Management Jump on the Data Base Wagon?" *Financial Executive* 47 (May 1979):24-30. **Management information systems, Information management.**

A modest but clear statement on definitions, advantages, and disadvantages of organizational data bases. Informative rather than prescriptive. A useful article.

Scott, George M. "A Data Base for Your Company?" *California Management Review* 19 (Fall 1976):68-78. **Management information systems, Organizational growth and change.**

An excellent primer on data base development and its relation to MIS. **Recommended.**

ELECTRONIC DATA PROCESSING

Bylinsky, Gene. "EDP Managers Put on Business Suits." *Fortune* 98 (October-December 1978):68. **Computer services, Managerial functions.**

A review of the role EDP managers play in several major corporations. This contains some interesting bits of information.

Foss, W. B. "Top Managers: What Do You Expect from EDP?" *Business Quarterly* 44 (Summer 1979):66-71. **Computer services, Management policy, strategy, and style.**

Another plea for top management involvement in EDP systems planning. It's all been said before.

Peck, Paul L. "Data Processing Safeguards." *Journal of Systems Management* 23 (October 1972):11-17. **Information processing, Computer services.**

A straightforward account of steps that can be taken to enhance the security of data processing hardware and software.

FUZZY SETS

Arbib, Michael A., and Manes, Ernest G. "A Category-Theoretic Approach to Systems in a Fuzzy World." *Synthèse* 30 (1975):381-406. **Systems theory.**

Technical, but a good discussion of the potential for control, i.e., the role knowledge of a future state plays in correcting the current state.

Bellman, R. E., and Zadeh, L. A. "Decision-Making in a Fuzzy Environment." *Management Science* 17 (December 1970):B141-64. **Decisionmaking, Operations research and management science.**

Technical but fascinating; the authors present one of the most profound advances in mathematical decision theory and computer science. A specific differentiation is made between *randomness* (probability) and *fuzziness*. **Recommended.**

Yager, Ronald, and Basson, David. "Decision Making with Fuzzy Sets." *Decision Sciences* 6 (July 1975):590-604. **Decisionmaking, Decision theory.**

A discussion and summary of Zadeh's work on fuzzy sets. Very technical, but worthwhile.

Zadeh, Lotfi A. "Outline of a New Approach to the Analysis of Complex Systems and Decision Processes." *IEEE Transactions on Systems, Man, and Cybernetics* SMC-3 (January 1973):28-44. **Analytical methods, Systems analysis.**

A very technical discussion; this is a powerful tool for dealing with complex systems and should be included in any serious attempt to deal with man-machine interfaces. The author is a pioneer in this field.

INFORMATION MANAGEMENT

Berlo, David K. "Right to Know, Need to Learn." *Personnel Administrator* 21 (November 1976):20. **Organization and management theory, Manager and controller roles.**

An excellent discussion of information control and management. Overload and communication are critical elements in managing knowledge and information flows. **Recommended.**

Branscomb, Lewis M. "Information: The Ultimate Frontier." *Science* 203 (12 January 1979):143-47. **Information systems.**

A good discussion of futurism, information, and computer technology. This is a good view of the role computers can and cannot play in the next hundred years.

Farmer, Richard N. *New Directions in Management Information Transfer.* Topics no. 7. Ruschlikon-Zurich, Switzerland: Gottlieb Duttweiler Institute for Economic and Social Studies, 1968. **Comparative management, Technology transfer.**

An intelligent appraisal of information management, with a comparative orientation. This article is suggestive and tentative rather than prescriptive and assertive.

Henry, Nicholas L. "Knowledge Management: A New Concern for Public Administration." *Public Administration Review* 34 (May-June 1974): 189-96. **Management in public organizations, Policy analysis.**

Information technology and public administration. This meandering article lacks focus.

Horton, Forest Woody, Jr. "Budgeting and Accounting for Information." *Government Accountants Journal* 28 (Spring 1979):21-31. **Management accounting, Accounting.**

A confusing proposal for *formally* budgeting and accounting for information. It is hard to dispute that information is a resource, but how to carry out the recommendations is a problem.

Kochen, Manfred, ed. *Information for Action: From Knowledge to Wisdom.* New York: Academic Press, 1975. **Information processing, Organization and management theory.**

There are sensible essays in this collection, but the overall framework of a world "brain," labeled WISE (World Information Synthesis and Encyclopedia), is fatuous.

Lacho, Kenneth J. "An Analysis of Information Search in Food Broker Product Mix Decisions." *Akron Business and Economic Review* 4 (Fall 1973):50-57. **Management effectiveness, Information processing.**

The article describes information search and decisionmaking in a highly competitive, uncertain business. Behavior is systematic and analytic, but not in the formal sense prescribed by "experts."

Muse, William V. "Information Sharing and Organizational Success." *Akron Business and Economic Review* 1 (1970):71-73. **Information processing, Organizational effectiveness.**

A weak study that contributes little to our understanding of the process described in the title.

Pearce, F. T. "Business Intelligence Systems: The Need, Development, and Integration." *Industrial Marketing Management* 5 (1976):115-38. **Organization and management theory, Decisionmaking.**

This article is too long, but there are some good points made. Although it suffers from a too-common conceptual confusion, it is worth a look.

Schofield, W. M. "GAO Reports Limited Success Controlling Regulatory Agencies' Demands for Paperwork from the Public." *Financial Executive* 45 (January 1977):32-35. **Management in public organizations, Bureaucracy.**

The GAO continues its battle with paperwork while generating lots of its own.

Weiss, E. C., ed. *The Many Faces of Information Science.* AAAS Selected Symposium 3. Boulder, Colo.: Westview Press, 1977. **Decisionmaking, Control systems and techniques.**

A mixed collection of papers on information science. Very formalistic, unreal, and confusing, this volume is only for the dedicated believer.

Wessel, Andrew E. *The Social Use of Information.* New York: John Wiley, 1976. **Information processing, Information systems.**

Wessel examines the many questions that arise as more and more information is stored and processed by high-speed systems. A combination of social and technical issues is raised and discussed, though not resolved. This is an intelligently modest approach.

Westin, Alan F., ed. *Information Technology in a Democracy.* Cambridge, Mass.: Harvard University Press, 1971. **Analytical methods, Information processing.**

This rough collection has a few essay gems in pages of tedium. In most cases, the good material has appeared elsewhere. This volume does give a reasonably good survey of general thinking on the subject through 1970. It is hard to tell how much has changed since then.

INFORMATION PROCESSING

Business Equipment Manufacturing Association. *Information Processing for Management.* Elmhurst, Ill.: The Business Press, 1969. **Computer services.**

A manufacturer's catalog of hardware and software. The volume is now obviously out of date, but it does give a perspective on how fast we have moved in so short a time.

Conference Board. *Information Technology.* New York: Conference Board, 1972. **Computer services.**

A compendium of the state of the art, 1972.

Dervin, Brenda. "Useful Theory for Librarianship: Communication, Not Information." *Drexel Library Quarterly* 13 (July 1977):16-32. **Organizational communication, Information systems.**

The focus is librarianship, but the argument is applicable to all information systems. A sensible, worthwhile article.

Dew, R. Beresford, and Gee, K. P. "Management Control Information: The Problem of Choice." *Management International Review* 10 (1970):63-68. **Information systems, Control systems and techniques.**

Some valuable data on information use in large organizations. The authors found that the popular conceptions of who values what information are mistaken. See their other work.

Huber, George P.; O'Connell, Michael J.; and Cummings, Larry L. "Perceived Environmental Uncertainty: Effects of Information and Structure." *Academy of Management Journal* 18 (December 1975):725-40. **Organizational structure, Risk and uncertainty.**

This article has a very narrow concentration, but the authors construct links to Duncan's work on perceived uncertainty and organizational structure. This has little utility except as a research note.

Kennedy, Miles H., and Mahapatra, Sitikantha. "Information Analysis for Effective Planning and Control." *Sloan Management Review* 16 (Winter 1975):71-83. **Control systems and techniques, Planning.**

A dogmatic article, of interest only to believers.

San Miguel, Joseph G. "Information Processing in Managerial Decision Making: A Preliminary Study." *Omega* 4 (1976):577-82. **Decision analysis, Decisionmaking.**

A speculative venture. Since undergraduate business students were the subject of the study, the results can hardly apply to *managerial* decisionmaking.

Snowball, Doug. "Information Load and Accounting Reports: Too Much, Too Little or Just Right?" *Cost and Management* 53 (May-June 1979): 22-28. **Accounting, Management information systems.**

A summary statement on the psychological and organizational implications of information overload.

Swieringa, Robert; Gibbins, Michael; Larsson, Lars; and Sweeney, Janet Lawson. "Experiments in the Heuristics of Human Information Processing." *Journal of Accounting Research* 14 (Supplement, 1976):159-95. **Decisionmaking, Accounting.**

An obtuse academic study. The authors present some good material on subjective probability, but the reader has to work for it.

INFORMATION SYSTEMS

Axelson, Charles F. "How to Avoid the Pitfalls of Information Systems Development." *Management Review* 65 (September 1976):47-51. **Organizational design, Organizational communication.**

A lightweight listing of principles and "commandments" that could be useful in examining assumptions about automated systems installation.

Cleland, David I. "Information Systems and Management Systems." In *Information Science: Search for Identity,* edited by Anthony Debons. New York: Marcel Dekker, 1974, pp. 313-26. **Management information systems, Control systems and techniques.**

Cleland assumes that MIS equals control, but there is nothing on where the information comes from or how it is filtered. Some discussion of informal organizational systems and control.

Hay, Leon E. "What Is an Information System?" *Business Horizons* 14 (February 1971):65-72. **Management effectiveness, Control systems and techniques.**

A formalistic statement in which the author doesn't clearly answer his own question.

Hayes, Robert L., and Radosevich, Raymond. "Designing Information Systems for Strategic Decisions." *Long Range Planning* 7 (August 1974): 45-48. **Decisionmaking.**

An argument for developing small information systems to support planning before moving to comprehensive systems. But planning is not knowing—it's just another way of guessing.

MacCrimmon, Kenneth R. "Descriptive Aspects of Team Theory: Observation, Communication and Decision Heuristics in Information Systems."

Edstrom, Anders. "User Influence and the Success of MIS Projects: A Contingency Approach." *Human Relations* 30 (1977):589-607. **Managerial functions, Control systems and techniques, Organization and management theory.**

A study of user effects on MIS success in France. It is not clear what the author means by success.

Ein-dor, Phillip, and Segev, Eli. "Information-System Responsibility." *MSU Business Topics* 25 (Autumn 1977):33-40. **Managerial functions, Control systems and techniques, Organization and management theory.**

Another review of user-system designer relationships and MIS success.

Elam, Phillip G. "User-Defined Information System Quality." *Journal of Systems Management* 30 (August 1979):30-33. **Control systems and techniques, Computer services.**

The title must sound familiar. More of the same.

Gallagher, Charles A. "Perceptions of the Value of a Management Information System." *Academy of Management Journal* 17 (March 1974):46-55. **Computer services, Control systems and techniques.**

A short report on a study of managers' perceptions of MIS. This is informative, but there are not enough data to be really useful.

Gartenberg, Morris, and Randall, Robert F. "From EDP to MIS and Beyond." *Management Accounting* 60 (April 1979):13-16. **Data processing, Management accounting.**

A lightweight, visionary promotional article, interesting because of the preoccupation with the control potential of MIS.

Getz, C. W. "MIS and the War Room." *Datamation* 23 (December 1977):66-70. **Control systems and techniques, Operations research and management science.**

A marvelous anachronistic statement arguing that management principles have not changed since Taylor et al. Control is everything. This should be read, if only to see what some senior people are willing to say in public.

Ghymn, Kyung, II, and King, William R. "Design of a Strategic Planning Management Information System." *Omega* 4 (1976):595-607. **Strategic planning, Decisionmaking.**

Another attempt to survey managers to find out, "Who needs what information?" The sample was hierarchically stratified and followed formal organizational patterns, so the conclusions are misleading.

Management Science 20 (June 1974):1323-34. **Decisionmaking, Organizational design.**

An interesting exercise that is primarily intended for an academic audience. Some probable use for technical systems managers.

Post, James E., and Epstein, Marc J. "Information Systems for Social Reporting." *Academy of Management Review* 2 (January 1977):81-87. **Policy analysis, Accounting.**

It is hard to tell what this is about. Lots of jargon but no substance.

Smith, C. Peter. "Resolving User/Systems Differences." *Journal of Systems Management* 28 (July 1977):16-21. **Organizational communication, Control systems and techniques.**

Another article on user/systems analyst conflict. This is more of the same.

MANAGEMENT INFORMATION SYSTEMS

Ackoff, Russell L. "Management Misinformation Systems." *Management Science* 14 (December 1967):B147-56. **Information processing, Control systems and techniques.**

This article has been severely criticized by MIS proponents and is now somewhat dated, but it is required reading simply because many of the problems Ackoff discusses still exist.

Adams, Carl R. "How Management Users View Information Systems." *Decision Sciences* 6 (April 1976):337-45. **Planning, Management policy, strategy, and style.**

A report on a survey of 75 functional managers and their views on MIS. The results are inconclusive, but there is repeated reference to managers' indifference, which is interpreted positively.

————, and Schroeder, Roger G. "Managers and MIS: 'They Get What They Want'." *Business Horizons* 16 (December 1973):63-68. **Management policy, strategy, and style, Management effectiveness.**

Another survey. Confusing conclusions are drawn from a small sample (N = 39) of mid-level managers. For example, "managers are looking for minor and . . . uninteresting improvements, such as accuracy and timing."

Argyris, Chris. "Management Information Systems: The Challenge to Rationality and Emotionality." *Management Science* 17 (February 1971):B275-92. **Organizational psychology, Personnel management.**

A socio-psychological perspective on MIS in organizations. The author sees a great need for "inter-personal competence" in implementing MIS.

————. "Organizational Learning and Effective Management Information Systems: A Prospectus for Research." Working Paper 76-4. Program on Information Technologies and Public Policy, Harvard University, May 1976. **Organizational learning, Organizational psychology.**

A longer version of Argyris's 1977 article in *Harvard Business Review* ("Double Loop Learning"). This piece, as a research prospectus, is particularly concerned with MIS as a control system, i.e., to detect and correct errors.

Alter, Steven L. "How Effective Managers Use Information Systems." *Harvard Business Review* 54 (November-December 1976):97-104. **Decisionmaking, Organization and management theory.**

A good analysis of the role MIS plays in various decisionmaking systems. There is the usual plea for more user involvement, but little on why some systems are more appropriate than others.

————, and Ginzberg, Michael. "Managing Uncertainty in MIS Implementation." *Sloan Management Review* 20 (Fall 1978):23-31. **Control systems and techniques, Analytical methods.**

A sensible MIS implementation strategy is outlined, but the call is still for user involvement. The question remains: How?

Banbury, John. "Information System Design, Organizational Control and Optimality." *Omega* 3 (1975):449-60. **Decisionmaking, Operations research and management science.**

Another framework for optimal MIS design, this is a plea for user/planner interaction to eliminate MIS adaptive shortcomings.

Beishon, R. J. "Information Flow and Manager's Decisions." *Management Accounting* (UK) 48 (November 1970):385-90. **Managerial functions, Information processing.**

A short critique of a narrow technical approach to information systems. The call is for more behavioral scientist involvement. "Everybody wants to get into the act."

Boulton, William R. "The Changing Requirements for Managing Corporate Information Systems." *MSU Business Topics* 26 (Summer 1978): 4-12. **Managerial functions, Organizational design, Control systems and techniques.**

A highly prescriptive argument for information systems to support the executive function. Little on how or why.

Cerullo, Michael J. "MIS: What Can Go Wrong?" *Management Accounting* 60 (April 1979):43-48. **Control systems and techniques, Management policy, strategy, and style.**

Another article decrying the lack of top management involvement in MIS. There is a message here somewhere.

Cerveny, Robert P.; Mahajan, Vijay; and Ludwig, Robert A. "Management Information Systems in Health Systems Agencies: Some Considerations." *Socio-Economic Planning Science* 12 (1978):229-36. **Management in public organizations, Policy analysis.**

MIS in public agencies. The authors argue that the system must be designed with organizational environment (constraints, personnel, etc.) in mind.

Coleman, Dr. Raymond J., and Riley, M.J. "The Organizational Impact of MIS." *Journal of Systems Management* 23 (March 1972):13-19. **Manager and controller roles, Organizational growth and change.**

Another call for managerial commitment to MIS. All the positive assumptions of MIS are accepted as fact, and resistance to change is the reason for lack of widespread use.

Dearden, John. "MIS Is a Mirage." *Harvard Business Review* 50 (January-February 1972):90-99. **Organizational design, Information systems.**

One of the best, this article should be required reading for all managers and MIS proponents. A bit dated, but still valuable. **Recommended.**

Dew, R. B., and Gee, K. P. *Management Control and Information: Studies in the Use of Control Information by Middle Management in Manufacturing Companies.* New York: John Wiley, 1973. **Information processing, Control systems and techniques.**

A full report of the Dew and Gee studies that appeared earlier as articles. This is one of the few efforts to systematically explore the actual *use* managers make of so-called control information.

Dickson, Gary W.; Senn, James A.; Chervany, Norman L. "Research in Management Information Systems: The Minnesota Experiments." *Management Science* 23 (May 1977):913-23. **Decisionmaking, Information processing.**

Report of an experimental study that came up with two not-so-startling findings: (1) information system *structure* affects decisions; and (2) personal attributes of the decisionmaker affects decisions.

————, and Simmons, John K. "The Behavioral Side of MIS." *Business Horizons* 13 (August 1970):59-71. **Personnel management, Organizational goals and objectives.**

Managing management information systems as a function of personnel reactions to MIS installation. Another plea for user orientation.

Diebold Group. *Investment in Management Information Systems, 19__.* Document No. M32. New York: The Diebold Group, December 19__. **Control systems and techniques.**

A journal report from the Diebold Group, interesting only in the view it offers of the potential of MIS.

Griffin, Marvin A. "Information Processing Systems." *AIIE Transactions* 8 (September 1976):307-13. **Information processing.**

This starts out as an intelligent discussion of the problems in matching specialist concerns with management tasks, but it winds up as another outline of a technical information processing model.

Gruenberger, Fred, ed. *Information Systems for Management*. Englewood Cliffs, N.J.: Prentice-Hall, 1972. **Information processing, Control systems and techniques.**

A good collection of essays dealing with various aspects of automated information systems. Not all of the experiences discussed are salutary.

Gul, Ferdinand A. K. "The Problem of Feedback in an MIS." *Management Accounting* (UK) 56 (February 1978):62-63. **Control systems and techniques, Information processing.**

A perfect illustration of a control system that is labeled "MIS." Feed-forward is added to feedback to make sure things go as planned. Brief nonsense.

Hanold, Terrance. "An Executive View of MIS." *Datamation* 18 (November 1972):65-71. **Information processing, Management policy, strategy, and style.**

This article tells how a system is used to move and mix flour, but there is not much on how Hanold actually uses the system to make decisions in uncertain situations.

Hershauer, James C. "What's Wrong with Systems Design Methods? It's Our Assumptions!" *Journal of Systems Management* 29 (April 1978): 25-28. **Computer services, Control systems and techniques.**

An examination of the assumptions underlying computer systems design. Unfortunately, the author uses diagrams instead of data to support his argument.

Higgins, J. C., and Finn, R. "The Chief Executive and His Information System." *Omega* 5 (1977):557-66. **Management policy, strategy, and style, Control systems and techniques.**

An interesting but inconclusive study; this is another questionnaire survey that does not deal with the question of what is *done* with all the reports the information system produces.

Horton, Forest W., Jr. "The Evolution of MIS in Government." *Journal of Systems Management* 25 (March 1974):14-20. **Management in public organizations, Information processing.**

A fairly good discussion of the problems that occur with an integrated MIS in a pluralistic organization that has many competing information systems. The prescription is like motherhood and apple pie.

Horton, Woody, Jr. "Budgeting the Data and Information Resource." *Journal of Systems Management* 28 (February 1977):12-14. **Management in public organizations.**

A wordy statement in pure bureaucratese.

Jain, Suresh K. "A Simulation-Based Scheduling and Management Information System for a Machine Shop." *Interfaces* 6 (November 1975): 81-96. **Control systems and techniques, Operations research and management science.**

An excellent account of the design of a control system, in which the design process itself was not treated as a control problem. This is also a good example of how "deviation," not the operator, signaled an error in the plan. There is little system in systems design. **Recommended.**

Johnson, Robert L., and Derman, Irwin H. "How Intelligent Is Your 'MIS'? A Complete System Is Worth the Money." *Business Horizons* 13 (February 1970):55-62. **Control systems and techniques, Decision theory.**

An example of the "total system" movement that is now generally ignored. *Sic transit gloria.*

Kashyap, R. N. "Management Information Systems for Corporate Planning and Control." *Long Range Planning* 5 (June 1972):25-31. **Control systems and techniques, Systems approach.**

A formalistic, prescriptive statement filled with superficial optimism. Not worth the trouble.

Kennedy, Miles H., and Mahapatra, Sitikantha. "Information Analysis for Effective Planning and Control." *Sloan Management Review* 17 (Winter 1975):71-83. **Problem solving, Information processing.**

An inconclusive study of managers' information sources and requirements. Some of the more interesting findings were non-quantifiable and were, therefore, not explored. A case of methodological straitjacketing.

Lawler, Edward E., III, and Rhode, John Grant. *Information and Control in Organizations.* Pacific Palisades, Calif.: Goodyear, 1976. **Control systems and techniques, Information processing.**

The total systems approach applied to organizational control. The authors are inconsistent in their conceptual and theoretical constructs, and their work is therefore confusing.

Lucas, Henry C., Jr. "An Empirical Study of a Framework for Information Systems." *Decision Sciences* 5 (January 1974):102-14. **Information management, Decisionmaking.**

A study that shows MIS as most useful in routine circumstances, when it has not yet penetrated the upper levels of the organizational hierarchy.

Management Science 20 (June 1974):1323-34. **Decisionmaking, Organizational design.**

An interesting exercise that is primarily intended for an academic audience. Some probable use for technical systems managers.

Post, James E., and Epstein, Marc J. "Information Systems for Social Reporting." *Academy of Management Review* 2 (January 1977):81-87. **Policy analysis, Accounting.**

It is hard to tell what this is about. Lots of jargon but no substance.

Smith, C. Peter. "Resolving User/Systems Differences." *Journal of Systems Management* 28 (July 1977):16-21. **Organizational communication, Control systems and techniques.**

Another article on user/systems analyst conflict. This is more of the same.

MANAGEMENT INFORMATION SYSTEMS

Ackoff, Russell L. "Management Misinformation Systems." *Management Science* 14 (December 1967):B147-56. **Information processing, Control systems and techniques.**

This article has been severely criticized by MIS proponents and is now somewhat dated, but it is required reading simply because many of the problems Ackoff discusses still exist.

Adams, Carl R. "How Management Users View Information Systems." *Decision Sciences* 6 (April 1976):337-45. **Planning, Management policy, strategy, and style.**

A report on a survey of 75 functional managers and their views on MIS. The results are inconclusive, but there is repeated reference to managers' indifference, which is interpreted positively.

————, and Schroeder, Roger G. "Managers and MIS: 'They Get What They Want'." *Business Horizons* 16 (December 1973):63-68. **Management policy, strategy, and style, Management effectiveness.**

Another survey. Confusing conclusions are drawn from a small sample (N = 39) of mid-level managers. For example, "managers are looking for minor and . . . uninteresting improvements, such as accuracy and timing."

Argyris, Chris. "Management Information Systems: The Challenge to Rationality and Emotionality." *Management Science* 17 (February 1971): B275-92. **Organizational psychology, Personnel management.**

A socio-psychological perspective on MIS in organizations. The author sees a great need for "inter-personal competence" in implementing MIS.

————. "Organizational Learning and Effective Management Information Systems: A Prospectus for Research." Working Paper 76-4. Program on Information Technologies and Public Policy, Harvard University, May 1976. **Organizational learning, Organizational psychology.**

A longer version of Argyris's 1977 article in *Harvard Business Review* ("Double Loop Learning"). This piece, as a research prospectus, is particularly concerned with MIS as a control system, i.e., to detect and correct errors.

Alter, Steven L. "How Effective Managers Use Information Systems." *Harvard Business Review* 54 (November-December 1976):97-104. **Decisionmaking, Organization and management theory.**

A good analysis of the role MIS plays in various decisionmaking systems. There is the usual plea for more user involvement, but little on why some systems are more appropriate than others.

————, and Ginzberg, Michael. "Managing Uncertainty in MIS Implementation." *Sloan Management Review* 20 (Fall 1978):23-31. **Control systems and techniques, Analytical methods.**

A sensible MIS implementation strategy is outlined, but the call is still for user involvement. The question remains: How?

Banbury, John. "Information System Design, Organizational Control and Optimality." *Omega* 3 (1975):449-60. **Decisionmaking, Operations research and management science.**

Another framework for optimal MIS design, this is a plea for user/planner interaction to eliminate MIS adaptive shortcomings.

Beishon, R. J. "Information Flow and Manager's Decisions." *Management Accounting* (UK) 48 (November 1970):385-90. **Managerial functions, Information processing.**

A short critique of a narrow technical approach to information systems. The call is for more behavioral scientist involvement. "Everybody wants to get into the act."

Boulton, William R. "The Changing Requirements for Managing Corporate Information Systems." *MSU Business Topics* 26 (Summer 1978): 4-12. **Managerial functions, Organizational design, Control systems and techniques.**

A highly prescriptive argument for information systems to support the executive function. Little on how or why.

Cerullo, Michael J. "MIS: What Can Go Wrong?" *Management Accounting* 60 (April 1979):43-48. **Control systems and techniques, Management policy, strategy, and style.**

Another article decrying the lack of top management involvement in MIS. There is a message here somewhere.

Cerveny, Robert P.; Mahajan, Vijay; and Ludwig, Robert A. "Management Information Systems in Health Systems Agencies: Some Considerations." *Socio-Economic Planning Science* 12 (1978):229-36. **Management in public organizations, Policy analysis.**

MIS in public agencies. The authors argue that the system must be designed with organizational environment (constraints, personnel, etc.) in mind.

Coleman, Dr. Raymond J., and Riley, M.J. "The Organizational Impact of MIS." *Journal of Systems Management* 23 (March 1972):13-19. **Manager and controller roles, Organizational growth and change.**

Another call for managerial commitment to MIS. All the positive assumptions of MIS are accepted as fact, and resistance to change is the reason for lack of widespread use.

Dearden, John. "MIS Is a Mirage." *Harvard Business Review* 50 (January-February 1972):90-99. **Organizational design, Information systems.**

One of the best, this article should be required reading for all managers and MIS proponents. A bit dated, but still valuable. **Recommended.**

Dew, R. B., and Gee, K. P. *Management Control and Information: Studies in the Use of Control Information by Middle Management in Manufacturing Companies.* New York: John Wiley, 1973. **Information processing, Control systems and techniques.**

A full report of the Dew and Gee studies that appeared earlier as articles. This is one of the few efforts to systematically explore the actual *use* managers make of so-called control information.

Dickson, Gary W.; Senn, James A.; Chervany, Norman L. "Research in Management Information Systems: The Minnesota Experiments." *Management Science* 23 (May 1977):913-23. **Decisionmaking, Information processing.**

Report of an experimental study that came up with two not-so-startling findings: (1) information system *structure* affects decisions; and (2) personal attributes of the decisionmaker affects decisions.

―――, and Simmons, John K. "The Behavioral Side of MIS." *Business Horizons* 13 (August 1970):59-71. **Personnel management, Organizational goals and objectives.**

Managing management information systems as a function of personnel reactions to MIS installation. Another plea for user orientation.

Diebold Group. *Investment in Management Information Systems, 1974.* Document No. M32. New York: The Diebold Group, December 1974. **Control systems and techniques.**

A journal report from the Diebold Group, interesting only in the view it offers of the potential of MIS.

Edstrom, Anders. "User Influence and the Success of MIS Projects: A Contingency Approach." *Human Relations* 30 (1977):589-607. **Managerial functions, Control systems and techniques, Organization and management theory.**

A study of user effects on MIS success in France. It is not clear what the author means by success.

Ein-dor, Phillip, and Segev, Eli. "Information-System Responsibility." *MSU Business Topics* 25 (Autumn 1977):33-40. **Managerial functions, Control systems and techniques, Organization and management theory.**

Another review of user-system designer relationships and MIS success.

Elam, Phillip G. "User-Defined Information System Quality." *Journal of Systems Management* 30 (August 1979):30-33. **Control systems and techniques, Computer services.**

The title must sound familiar. More of the same.

Gallagher, Charles A. "Perceptions of the Value of a Management Information System." *Academy of Management Journal* 17 (March 1974): 46-55. **Computer services, Control systems and techniques.**

A short report on a study of managers' perceptions of MIS. This is informative, but there are not enough data to be really useful.

Gartenberg, Morris, and Randall, Robert F. "From EDP to MIS and Beyond." *Management Accounting* 60 (April 1979):13-16. **Data processing, Management accounting.**

A lightweight, visionary promotional article, interesting because of the preoccupation with the control potential of MIS.

Getz, C. W. "MIS and the War Room." *Datamation* 23 (December 1977):66-70. **Control systems and techniques, Operations research and management science.**

A marvelous anachronistic statement arguing that management principles have not changed since Taylor et al. Control is everything. This should be read, if only to see what some senior people are willing to say in public.

Ghymn, Kyung, II, and King, William R. "Design of a Strategic Planning Management Information System." *Omega* 4 (1976):595-607. **Strategic planning, Decisionmaking.**

Another attempt to survey managers to find out, "Who needs what information?" The sample was hierarchically stratified and followed formal organizational patterns, so the conclusions are misleading.

Griffin, Marvin A. "Information Processing Systems." *AIIE Transactions* 8 (September 1976):307-13. **Information processing.**

This starts out as an intelligent discussion of the problems in matching specialist concerns with management tasks, but it winds up as another outline of a technical information processing model.

Gruenberger, Fred, ed. *Information Systems for Management.* Englewood Cliffs, N.J.: Prentice-Hall, 1972. **Information processing, Control systems and techniques.**

A good collection of essays dealing with various aspects of automated information systems. Not all of the experiences discussed are salutary.

Gul, Ferdinand A. K. "The Problem of Feedback in an MIS." *Management Accounting* (UK) 56 (February 1978):62-63. **Control systems and techniques, Information processing.**

A perfect illustration of a control system that is labeled "MIS." Feedforward is added to feedback to make sure things go as planned. Brief nonsense.

Hanold, Terrance. "An Executive View of MIS." *Datamation* 18 (November 1972):65-71. **Information processing, Management policy, strategy, and style.**

This article tells how a system is used to move and mix flour, but there is not much on how Hanold actually uses the system to make decisions in uncertain situations.

Hershauer, James C. "What's Wrong with Systems Design Methods? It's Our Assumptions!" *Journal of Systems Management* 29 (April 1978): 25-28. **Computer services, Control systems and techniques.**

An examination of the assumptions underlying computer systems design. Unfortunately, the author uses diagrams instead of data to support his argument.

Higgins, J. C., and Finn, R. "The Chief Executive and His Information System." *Omega* 5 (1977):557-66. **Management policy, strategy, and style, Control systems and techniques.**

An interesting but inconclusive study; this is another questionnaire survey that does not deal with the question of what is *done* with all the reports the information system produces.

Horton, Forest W., Jr. "The Evolution of MIS in Government." *Journal of Systems Management* 25 (March 1974):14-20. **Management in public organizations, Information processing.**

A fairly good discussion of the problems that occur with an integrated MIS in a pluralistic organization that has many competing information systems. The prescription is like motherhood and apple pie.

Horton, Woody, Jr. "Budgeting the Data and Information Resource." *Journal of Systems Management* 28 (February 1977):12-14. **Management in public organizations.**

A wordy statement in pure bureaucratese.

Jain, Suresh K. "A Simulation-Based Scheduling and Management Information System for a Machine Shop." *Interfaces* 6 (November 1975): 81-96. **Control systems and techniques, Operations research and management science.**

An excellent account of the design of a control system, in which the design process itself was not treated as a control problem. This is also a good example of how "deviation," not the operator, signaled an error in the plan. There is little system in systems design. **Recommended.**

Johnson, Robert L., and Derman, Irwin H. "How Intelligent Is Your 'MIS'? A Complete System Is Worth the Money." *Business Horizons* 13 (February 1970):55-62. **Control systems and techniques, Decision theory.**

An example of the "total system" movement that is now generally ignored. *Sic transit gloria.*

Kashyap, R. N. "Management Information Systems for Corporate Planning and Control." *Long Range Planning* 5 (June 1972):25-31. **Control systems and techniques, Systems approach.**

A formalistic, prescriptive statement filled with superficial optimism. Not worth the trouble.

Kennedy, Miles H., and Mahapatra, Sitikantha. "Information Analysis for Effective Planning and Control." *Sloan Management Review* 17 (Winter 1975):71-83. **Problem solving, Information processing.**

An inconclusive study of managers' information sources and requirements. Some of the more interesting findings were non-quantifiable and were, therefore, not explored. A case of methodological straitjacketing.

Lawler, Edward E., III, and Rhode, John Grant. *Information and Control in Organizations.* Pacific Palisades, Calif.: Goodyear, 1976. **Control systems and techniques, Information processing.**

The total systems approach applied to organizational control. The authors are inconsistent in their conceptual and theoretical constructs, and their work is therefore confusing.

Lucas, Henry C., Jr. "An Empirical Study of a Framework for Information Systems." *Decision Sciences* 5 (January 1974):102-14. **Information management, Decisionmaking.**

A study that shows MIS as most useful in routine circumstances, when it has not yet penetrated the upper levels of the organizational hierarchy.

———. *Why Information Systems Fail.* New York: Columbia University Press, 1975. **Control systems and techniques, Information processing.**

The author is an MIS proponent, so the reasons for failure are presented as extra-systemic. Yet, unless management information systems can be designed to be used, they have little utility.

———. "Performance and the Use of an Information System." *Management Science* 21 (April 1975):908-19. **Organizational behavior, Information management.**

An attempt to identify how closely MIS use and organizational performance are correlated. The resulting correlation is very weak, but more research is needed.

———. "The Evolution of an Information System: From Key-Man to Every Person." *Sloan Management Review* 19 (Winter 1978):39-52. **Information management, Organizational growth and change.**

A suggested design approach to MIS implementation. The problem is still to get users involved.

Lusk, Edward J., and Wolf, Arthur E. "The Planning Dimension of a Data Base Information System." *Managerial Planning* 23 (January-February 1975):34-40. **Control systems and techniques, Data bases.**

An example of vacuous prescriptions, the authors are still calling for a "total" data base system in 1975.

Makridakis, Spyros G., and Wheelwright, S. C. "Cybernetic Oriented MIS." *Management International Review* 14 (1974):45-58. **Control systems and techniques, Information processing.**

A grand view of MIS that is slightly out of phase; most of the comprehensive arguments have been abandoned. But obviously hope springs eternal.

Mandell, S.L. "The Management Information System Is Going to Pieces." *California Management Review* 17 (Summer 1975):50-56. **Information processing, Computer services.**

A critique of centralized information processing, Mandell suggests that decentralized, strategically placed mini-computers are more likely to be integrated into organizational processes than centrally controlled large systems.

Mason, Richard O., and Moskowitz, Herbert. "Conservatism in Information Processing: Implications for Management Information Systems." *Decision Sciences* 3 (October 1972):35-54. **Decisionmaking, Information processing.**

An experiment in subjective probability that compares actual responses with revisions calculated by Baye's theorem. Very technical, but potentially useful in revising models of decisionmaking.

Meldman, Jeffrey A. "A New Technique for Modeling the Behavior of Man-Machine Information Systems." *Sloan Management Review* 18 (Spring 1977):29-46. **Modeling and simulation, Analytical methods.**

More circles, squares, and arrows. This time it's "Petri nets," whose utility remains unproven.

Mintzberg, Henry. "The Myths of MIS." *California Management Review* 15 (Fall 1972):92-97. **Managerial functions, Organization and management theory.**

A short but worthwhile statement that compares actual management tasks with the myths sustained by "total" information systems.

Mitroff, Ian I.; Nelson, John; and Mason, Richard O. "On Management Myth-Info Systems." *Management Science* 21 (December 1974):371-82. **Decision models, Risk and uncertainty.**

An interesting paper that examines the use of "stories" as information units and the role they play in problem solving and decisionmaking.

Moskowitz, Herbert, and Mason, Richard D. "Accounting for the Man-Information Interface in Management Information Systems." *Omega* 1 (November 1973):679-94. **Decisionmaking, Information processing.**

A technical effort to integrate psychological dimensions into mathematical models of information processing and use.

————, and Murnighan, John Keith. "Information Centralization of Organizational Information Structures via Reports of Exceptions." *Journal of Business Research* 4 (May 1976):145-62. **Organizational design, Decision theory.**

A technical discussion of questionable utility to any but the most arcane methodological researcher. Business school students are fast overtaking psychology undergraduates as research subjects.

Munro, Malcolm C. "Determining the Manager's Information." *Journal of Systems Management* 29 (June 1978):34-39. **Decision analysis, Decisionmaking.**

A vacuous statement that does nothing to help managers, "information analysts," or those of us interested in these functions.

Page, John R., and Hooper, H. Paul. "Basics of Information Systems Development." *Journal of Systems Management* 30 (August 1979): 12-16. **Control systems and techniques, Computer services.**

It seems amazing that this sort of thing is still written and published, when most systems experts long ago agreed that the "total" system does not and probably never will be designed and implemented.

Percy, Edgar A. "Incremental Improvement of a Community Mental Health Center Management Information System." *Evaluation* 4 (1977): 205-207. **Incrementalism, Policy analysis.**

A short account of how incremental (vs. comprehensive) improvements in a computerized system were carried out.

Powers, Richard F., and Dickson, Gary W. "MisProject Management: Myths, Opinions, and Reality." *California Management Review* 15 (Spring 1973):147-56. **Control systems and techniques, Project management.**

An excellent empirical examination of how MIS projects fit into organizational activities. But the call is still for more user involvement.

Reeves, Gary R., and Bussom, Robert S. "Information Systems Curriculum." *Journal of Systems Management* 30 (March 1979):18-21. **Management education and training.**

Another self-serving survey of MIS corporate use. There are a lot of numbers and few ideas in this exercise.

Sadek, Konrad E., and Tomeski, Edward A. "Future Challenges for MIS." *Journal of Systems Management* 30 (July 1979):30-35. **Control systems and techniques, Information management.**

A feeble argument for a partial return to the "total systems" (now called "macro") approach of the sixties.

Said, Kamal E. A. "MIS for Problem Detection, Diagnosis, and Evaluation." *Managerial Planning* 26 (March-April 1978):4-8. **Problem solving, Modeling and simulation.**

Confused metaphor equals problematic model. The author would have organizations behaving as machines with properties of an organism. How?

Schewe, Charles D., and Dillon, William R. "Marketing Information System Utilization: An Application of Self-Concept Theory." *Journal of Business Research* 6 (January 1978):67-79. **Information processing, Management policy, strategy, and style.**

Another study of system designer-user discontinuity. A plea is made (again) for more user involvement.

————, and Wiek, James L. "Innovative Strategies for Improving MIS Utilization." *Academy of Management Review* 2 (January 1977):138-42. **Information processing, Management effectiveness.**

The same as the other articles that promote management information systems. Skip it.

———. "Guide to MIS User Satisfaction." *Journal of Systems Management* 28 (June 1977):6-10. **Information processing, Management policy, strategy, and style.**

Users are not satisfied and must therefore be more involved in systems design.

Schneyman, Arthur H. "Management Information Systems for Management Sciences." *Interfaces* 6 (May 1976):52-59. **Operations research and management science, Control systems and techniques.**

MIS for MS? Lots of acronyms, charts, and tables, but not much substance.

Schonberger, Richard J., and Buterbaugh, Terry. "Management Information Systems in Pittsburgh Business Firms." *Pittsburgh Business Review* 46 (Winter 1976):1-4. **Data bases, Information processing.**

A study that pronounces the end of the electronic data processing (EDP) era and heralds the beginning of the MIS-data base era. But the study also reveals an inward *process*-oriented direction by systems specialists. What about users?

Schroeder, Roger G., and Benbasat, Izak. "An Experimental Evaluation of the Relationship of Uncertainty in the Environment to Information Used by Decision Makers." *Decision Sciences* 6 (July 1975):556-67. **Decisionmaking, Information processing, Risk and uncertainty.**

An interesting experiment in information use and uncertainty avoidance. The subjects used buffering tactics, and more information did not necessarily lead to better decisions.

Siegel, Paul. *Strategic Planning of Management Information Systems.* New York: Mason and Lipscomb, 1975. **Information processing, Planning.**

The usual MIS cant, with formal prescriptive models for installation.

Shio, Martin J. "New Look at MIS." *Journal of Systems Management* 28 (May 1977):38-40. **Control systems and techniques, Management effectiveness.**

More "how-to" prescriptions for MIS. The same problems continually come up; maybe there's a message in this, but it's being ignored.

Soden, John V. "Understanding MIS Failures." *Data Management* 13 (July 1975):29. **Information processing, Control systems and techniques.**

The general conclusion (not explicitly addressed) is that management information systems fail because we don't know very much about how they function.

———, and Tucker, Charles C. "Long Range MIS Planning." *Journal of*

Systems Management 27 (July 1976):28-33. **Long-range planning, Computer services.**

An interesting catalog of the pervasive ignorance in MIS installation and evaluation. The authors, however, seem completely unaware of uncertainty; their assertions carry the ring of revealed truth.

Sollenberger, Harold M. "Management Information Systems in the Real World." *Management Services* 6 (November-December 1969):30-37. **Computer services, Control systems and techniques.**

A somewhat dated but still valid critique of the unfulfilled promises of comprehensive computer systems.

Spencer, William I. "What Do Upper Executives Want from MIS?" *Administrative Management* 39 (July 1978):26. **Management, policy, strategy, and style, Organizational design.**

The answer provided (twice) by the author is information "to produce an infallible management decision . . . , at the least possible cost." No wonder MIS designers are always complaining they're being asked to deliver what was promised.

Sprague, Ralph H., Jr., and Watson, Hugh J. "MIS Concepts, Part 1." *Journal of Systems Management* 26 (January 1975):34-37. "Part 2." 26 (February 1975):35-40. **Decision analysis, Organization and management theory.**

An article that preaches the integrated MIS embedded in a hierarchical decision process for "strategic," "tactical," and "operational" decisions. The authors assume a data base that is comprehensive enough to serve all levels and all functions to eliminate suboptimizing.

Spurgat, Frederick A. *A Comparative Study of the Implementation and Use of Management Information Systems in a Federal Research Agency: Factors Affecting User Acceptance.* Ph.D. dissertation, Northwestern University, 1976. Ann Arbor, Mich.: Xerox University Microfilms, 1976. **Control systems and techniques, Management in public organizations.**

This is the only systematic study of MIS use that could be located. It's hard going, but there are some very interesting findings. Namely, "While enormous organizational resources, . . . are being dedicated to these systems, the intended users accept, stymie, block, sabotage, or simply ignore these systems." This is not the definitive study, but it certainly is a start. Others are needed.

Stout, Larry D. "The Problems of Management Information Systems: Why They Fail." *GAO Review* (Spring-Fall 1972), pp. 40-45. **Planning, Organizational growth and change.**

Another explanation of why management information systems fail.

Swanson, E. Burton. "Management Information Systems: Appreciation and Involvement." *Management Science* 21 (October 1974):178-88. **Management control, Control systems and techniques.**

Another argument for managerial involvement in MIS, with not much about how managers really use it.

————. "The Two Faces of Organizational Information." *Accounting, Organizations and Society* 3 (1978):237-46. **Organizational learning, Organizational effectiveness.**

A scrambled but interesting discussion of information in organizations. I am not quite sure where the argument leads, and the author doesn't provide much help. There is no examination of the implications of his description (not theory) for organizations.

Tricker, R. I. *Management Information and Control Systems.* London: John Wiley, 1976. **Control systems and techniques.**

A formalistic casebook for use as a text. It reads like a catechism; a ritual devoid of any sense of inquiry.

van Horn, Richard L. "Empirical Studies of Management Information Systems." *Data Base* 5 (Winter 1973):172-82. **Information processing, Analytical methods.**

A review of MIS research, with an interesting series of comments.

Walsh, Myles E. "MIS—Where Are We, How Did We Get Here, and Where Are We Going?" *Journal of Systems Management* 29 (November 1978):6-21. **Data bases, Electronic data processing.**

A fairly good explanation of data base technology. The author is in business, but he is not "selling" anything. Worth a look.

————. "Look Out Management—Here They Come Again." *Journal of Systems Management* 30 (July 1979):14-17. **Control systems and techniques, Computer services.**

An astute comparison of the heralded impact of word processors and mini computers with the MIS ballyhoo of the sixties. Good reading.

Watson, Hugh J.; Sprague, Ralph H., Jr.; and Kroeber, Donald W. "Computer Technology and Information System Performance." *MSU Business Topics* 25 (Summer 1977):17-24. **Computer services, Decisionmaking.**

Another "framework for conceptualizing" information systems.

Weinwurm, George F. "Managing Management Information." *Management International Review* 10 (1970):43-47. **Information management, Information processing.**

A short discussion of the vagaries of central computer-based information systems. Another listing of what should and should not be done.

Weiss, W. H. "Improving Your MIS." *Administrative Management* 37 (September 1976):56-58. **Control systems and techniques, Information processing.**

Some outrageous claims for MIS. Again, if an organization meets the criteria for successful MIS installation, who needs it?

West, Glenn M. "MIS in Small Companies." *Journal of Systems Management* 26 (April 1975):10-13. **Problem solving, Control systems and techniques.**

A trivial piece that counsels "a successful MIS is possible if the approach to the problem is correct." Under those conditions, *anything* is possible.

Willoughby, T. C., and Pye, Richard A. "Top Management's Computer Role." *Journal of Systems Management* 28 (September 1977):10-13. **Computer services, Managerial functions.**

Managers (users) and information systems again. If users are involved, the systems are better. Sound familiar?

Zachman, John A. "Control and Planning of Information Systems." *Journal of Systems Management* 28 (July 1977):34-41. **Control systems and techniques, Planning.**

Another plea for "top-down" planning in designing and controlling information systems.

MODELING AND SIMULATION

Boguslaw, Robert, and Davis, Robert H. "Social Process Modeling: A Comparison of a Live and Computerized Simulation." *Behavioral Science* 14 (1969):197-203. **Decisionmaking, Policy analysis.**

An interesting exercise in human and computer simulation of decisionmaking. This is somewhat dated technically, but there are some timeless comments on decisionmaking.

Gross, P. F. "Computers, Policymaking, and Reality." *Policy Sciences* 2 (June 1971):87-93. **Policy analysis, Planning.**

A critique of the computer's utility in health planning in the U.S. Some useful information and analysis.

Simon, J. C. "Complexity Concepts and the Limitations of Computable Models." *Technological Forecasting and Social Change* 13 (1979):1-11. **Computer services, Analytical methods.**

A discussion of language, complexity, and computers. This is interesting, but not for the layman.

Watt, Kenneth F. "Why Won't Anyone Believe Us?" *Simulation* 28 (January 1977):1-3. **Decisionmaking, Policy analysis.**

The title says it all—by a developer of large-scale computer simulations of society. It costs a lot so it must be good.

Control

CONTROL SYSTEMS AND TECHNIQUES

Anthony, Robert N. *Planning and Control Systems: A Framework for Analysis.* Boston: Graduate School of Business Administration, Harvard University, 1965. **Planning, Organization and management theory.**

One of the classics in the field, this volume should be read as an aid in understanding the confusion of management with control.

Axelson, Kenneth S. "Municipal Accounting: A Better Blueprint via IFMS." *Journal of Accountancy* 142 (December 1976):42-52. **Management in public organizations, Management accounting.**

An interview outlining the fiscal wonders possible with an Integrated Financial Management System (IFMS). Given the fiscal problems of the city where it was installed—New York—other municipalities should look carefully before leaping.

Baker, Donald W.; Barrett, Michael J.; and Radde, Leon R. "Top-Management Fraud: Something Can Be Done Now!" *Internal Auditor* 33 (October 1976):25-33. **Budgeting, Auditing.**

Auditors as *the* ideal control means in organizations. The authors make simplistic assumptions about managers, organizations, and the pervasiveness of fraud (evil) in corporations.

Belden, T. G. *Studies of Command and Control.* Study No. 2: *The Language of Command.* NTIS Report No. AD-425822. Alexandria, Va.: Institute for Defense Analyses, Research and Engineering Support Division, August 1962.

Part of a series outlining the potential for command and control systems in military applications. This is a good introduction to the concepts of command and control in other organizations.

Clutterbuck, David. "Out with Systems, in with Profitability." *International Management* 33 (November 1978):39. **Organizational growth and change, Computer services.**

A Canadian manufacturer's experience with complex computer systems that were not needed. "Simplify, simplify" seems to be sound advice in this case.

Dewelt, Robert L. "Control: Key to Making Financial Strategy Work." *Management Review* 66 (March 1977):18-25. **Planning, Evaluation and program effectiveness.**

A trite, ritualistic recitation of most of the misunderstandings and misperceptions of the managerial function.

Hampton, David R. "The Planning-Motivation Dilemma: Limitations and Advantages of Setting Goals." *Business Horizons* 16 (June 1973):79-87. **Organizational goals and objectives, Planning.**

Part of the PERT mythology. There is no discussion of the problems in closed-system control methods.

Hertz, David B. *New Power for Management: Computer Systems and Management Science.* New York: McGraw-Hill, 1969. **Operations research and management science, Computer services.**

Another statement on the control power now available through management science and computer applications. The question of who is to wield this power is not addressed.

Herzlinger, Regina. "Why Data Systems in Nonprofit Organizations Fail." *Harvard Business Review* 55 (January-February 1977):81-86. **Management information systems, Management in public organizations.**

"Bad" managers in public agencies cause control system failures in not-for-profit agencies. If they used the systems they would be "good." There is some problem here.

Hoffman, R. Randall. "MJS: Management by Job Standards." *Personnel Journal* 58 (August 1979):536-40. **Management by objectives, Personnel management.**

MBO tightened up and tied to performance—with evaluation and standards procedures. Process ascendant over substance.

Horovitz, J. H. "Strategic Control: A New Task for Top Management." *Long Range Planning* 12 (June 1979):2-7. **Comparative management, Planning.**

Report of an empirical study showing that long-range strategic controls are not present. The author argues that they *should* be.

Inohara, Hideo. "Transferring 'Foreign' Ideas: The Zero Defects Movement in Japan." *European Business,* no. 37 (Spring 1973), pp. 62-68. **Technology transfer, Error detection and correction.**

An account of how a perfection-oriented U.S. system was installed in Japan and then adapted to fit existing management practice. Good idea; it happens in the U.S., too, only we are not so quick to acknowledge that it does.

Kennedy, Miles H. "Real Time vs. Exception Reports." *Journal of Systems Management* 25 (April 1974):22-26. **Information processing, Management information systems.**

This article has more discussion of response lags (including diagnosis and implementation), false alarms, and other problems in information systems than is usually encountered.

Kim, Chaiho. "Decomposition of Planning Systems." *Decision Sciences* 1 (July-October 1970):397-422. **Decision analysis, Planning.**

A computational exercise requiring great precision, but the author begins with guesswork. Unless algorithms are valued for their own sake, it is hard to see how such exercises can help anyone.

Lowe, E. A. "On the Idea of Management Control System: Integrating Accounting and Management Control." *Journal of Management Studies* 8 (February 1971):1-12. **Management control, Accounting.**

A prime example of the management control confusion. The author makes only a minor contextual distinction and then goes on to a noncontextual evaluation of decision strategies. Confusing.

Machol, Robert E. "Principles of Operations Research." *Interfaces* 4 (May 1974):26-27. **Operations research and management science, Analytical methods.**

Part of a series, this is a short but effective statement on "solutions looking for problems."

Morgenstern, Oskar. "The Command and Control Structure." Research Memorandum no. 47. Princeton University Econometric Research Program, October 1962, pp. 1-25. **Organizational control, Systems analysis.**

An elegant statement on military command and control systems. This is useful reading for those contemplating similar designs.

Picard, Jacques. "How European Companies Control Marketing Decisions Abroad." *Columbia Journal of World Business* 12 (Summer 1977):113-21. **Comparative management, Decisionmaking.**

A research report on control patterns in headquarters/subsidiary operations. Control imposed varies with the uncertainty of the domain and is strongest in budgeting.

Purcell, John, and Earl, Michael J. "Control Systems and Industrial Relations." *Industrial Relations Journal* 8 (1977):41-54. **Management control.**

The authors propose a control system for industrial relations; but it's not really a *control* system, it's an attention direction device. Is this management by exception? This article is worth looking at because of the author's conceptual confusion.

Reuter, Vincent G. "Using Graphic Management Tools." *Journal of Systems Management* 30 (April 1979):6-17. **PERT and CPM.**

Another article that assumes the efficacy of closed-system control techniques. The author finds use "encouraging," and wider use would be even better! There is no mention of task environment.

Roberts, Edward B., ed. *Managerial Applications of System Dynamics.* Cambridge, Mass.: The MIT Press, 1978. **Modeling and simulations, Systems theory.**

A massive volume, containing reports and essays of those associated with the MIT group of comprehensive system modelers (Jay W. Forrester is perhaps the best-known member). The book is most valuable as a state-of-the-art summary, though the papers are not all new (Herbert A. Simon's is from 1952). Interesting if you're interested, otherwise tedious and trivial.

Sayles, Leonard. "The Many Dimensions of Control." *Organizational Dynamics* 1 (Summer 1972):21-31. **Manager and controller roles, Managerial functions.**

The interplay of task, organization, and environment in designing control systems. The referent is the U.S. National Aeronautics and Space Administration (NASA).

Turcotte, William E. "Control Systems, Performance, and Satisfaction in Two State Agencies." *Administrative Science Quarterly* 19 (March 1974):60-73. **Bureaucracy, Organizational effectiveness.**

An excellent study indicating that tight control systems do *not* improve organizational performance. Personal and financial measures of satisfaction and success are used. **Recommended.**

Wiener, Norbert. *Cybernetics.* New York: John Wiley, 1948. **Information processing, Systems approach.**

The classic work by the inventor of *cybernetics* —the term and the approach. Unfortunately, it often seems that modern proponents have not yet read Wiener.

———. *The Human Use of Human Beings.* New York: Avon, 1967. **Systems approach, Computer services.**

This is Wiener's reaction to his growing awareness of the potential for misuse of computer technology and cybernetic principles. This book is popular with many anti-computer zealots, but it was not intended to serve that purpose. It is a sensible plea for knowledge preceding prescription.

Youssef, Samir M. "Contextual Factors Influencing Control Strategy of Multinational Corporations." *Academy of Management Journal* 18 (March 1975):136-43. **Organizational effectiveness, Organizational goals and objectives.**

A trite and useless discussion of control in multinational corporations.

INVENTORY CONTROL

Gibson, D. W., and Butler, J. E. "Evaluation of Inventory Management: Efficiency Can Affect Success." *Business Horizons* 16 (June 1973):51-60. **Control systems and techniques, Management models.**

An honest statement outlining the application and limitations of a management science model. The author addresses the information needs demanded by the model.

Reuter, Vincent G. "ABC Method to Inventory Control." *Journal of Systems Management* 27 (November 1976):26-33. **Control systems and techniques.**

The "vital few and trivial many" concepts of Pareto's law is applied to the inventory control process. The author presents a lot of detail, but the article's utility is questionable.

MANAGEMENT CONTROL

Gilbert, Xavier F. "Does Your Control System Fit Your Firm?" *European Business,* no. 37 (Spring 1973), pp. 69-76. **Control systems and techniques, Management policy, strategy, and style.**

The author extols the virtues of management control systems without seriously questioning or examining the premises on which such systems are based.

Hofstede, Geert. "The Poverty of Management Control Philosophy." *Academy of Management Review* 3 (July 1978):450-61. **Planning, programming, and budgeting, Control systems and techniques.**

A good examination of the problems inherent in cybernetic models of organizational control. Hofstede specifically addresses failures of

Planning-Programming-Budgeting (PPB) and management by objectives.

Hughes, R. Eugene. "Planning: The Essence of Control." *Managerial Planning* 26 (May-June 1978):1. **Planning, Organizational effectiveness.**

A good example of the emphasis placed on control concerns in the organization and management literature. This is short and not very original.

Jarvis, Bill, and Skidmore, Derek. "The Accountant and the Control Process in Business." *Accountancy* 89 (September 1978):99-100. **Control systems and techniques, Management accounting.**

An example of how control processes in businesses are viewed by some accountants. No ambiguity here: "The aim should be to optimise the total amount of control in the organization."

Kinnunen, Raymond M., and Caplan, Robert H., III. "The Domain of Management Control." *University of Michigan Business Review* 30 (May 1978):1-9. **Organizational behavior.**

A formalistic, jargon-filled article of little use to anyone.

Lorange, Peter. "A Framework for Management Control Systems." *Sloan Management Review* 16 (Fall 1974):41-56. **Control systems, Organizational goals and objectives.**

An interesting discussion; this is an excellent presentation of how management control systems can become ends in themselves and displace organizational goals. Good bibliography.

Lowe, E. A., and McInnes, J. M. "Control in Socio-Economic Organizations: A Rationale for the Design of Management Control Systems (Section I)." *Journal of Management Studies* 8 (May 1971):213-27. **Systems analysis.**

A cryptic statement with a number of complex diagrams but little new information. I could not locate Section II in following issues of the journal; the MCS apparently didn't work.

Ouchi, William G., and Dowling, John B. "Defining the Span of Control." *Administrative Science Quarterly* 19 (1974):357-65. **Personnel management, Organization and management theory.**

An exercise in manipulating a meaningless classical management "principle."

Sihler, William H. "Toward Better Management Control Systems." *California Management Review* 13 (Winter 1971):33-39. **Organizational structure, Information systems.**

An example of the trite, vacuous, cliché-ridden claptrap that gets published.

Todd, John. "Management Control Systems: A Key Link Between Strategy, Structure and Employee Performance." *Organizational Dynamics* 5 (Spring 1977):65-78. **Control systems and techniques, Personnel management.**

An outline of a flexible management control system. The model of cybernetic control is linked to employee performance and potential rather than automatic (self-correcting) control, as in financial accounting.

Vancil, Richard F. "What Kind of Management Control Do You Need?" *Harvard Business Review* 51 (March-April 1973):75-86. **Organizational design, Organizational structure.**

Another instance where control equals management; it is just a matter of understanding the formal structure.

Wildavsky, Aaron. "Does Planning Work?" *Public Interest* 72 (Summer 1971):95-104. **Planning, Economic development.**

A review essay that makes some good points on the utility of planning as an organizational and national activity.

ORGANIZATIONAL CONTROL

Jacobs, David. "Dependency and Vulnerability: An Exchange Approach to the Control of Organizations." *Administrative Science Quarterly* 19 (March 1974):44-59. **Organizational behavior, Organizational effectiveness.**

A muddled use of the concept of control produces confusion in an otherwise interesting discussion of organizational environments.

McMahon, J. Timothy, and Perritt, G. W. "The Control Structure of Organizations: An Empirical Examination." *Academy of Management Journal* 14 (September 1971):327-39. **Organizational structure, Control systems and techniques.**

A trivial methodological critique of others' work. It is hardly worth the trouble.

Miner, John B. "The Uncertain Future of the Leadership Concept: An Overview." *Organization and Administrative Sciences* 6 (Summer-Fall 1975):197-208. **Management policy, strategy, and style, Management effectiveness.**

A good deal of conceptual ambiguity leaves the reader uncertain as to what the author is saying.

Ouchi, William G. "The Transmission of Control Through Organizational Hierarchy." *Academy of Management Journal* 21 (June 1978):173-92. **Control systems and techniques.**

Another examination of output and behavior control. This time the focus is on hierarchic transmission. There is still no clarification of the concept of *control*, but "control is assumed to be unidirectional from the top down."

————, and Maguire, Mary Ann. "Organizational Control: Two Functions." *Administrative Science Quarterly* 20 (December 1975):559-69. **Control systems and techniques.**

An empirical examination of "behavior" vs. "output" control in organizations. The authors further obscure the meaning of control, but it is a useful exercise.

Tannenbaum, Arnold S. *Control in Organizations.* New York: McGraw-Hill, 1968. **Control systems and techniques.**

An extensive examination of the concept of control in organizational systems. Since control is so often the prescription offered for organizations, this work should be included in any serious reading program.

Decision

BARGAINING AND NEGOTIATION

Lane, Tracy, and Peterson, Richard B. "Tackling Problems Through Negotiation." *Human Resource Management* 18 (Summer 1979):14-23. **Problem solving, Organizational behavior.**

A good correlational analysis of bargaining/negotiation behaviors and problem-solving activity. This is one of the few efforts aimed at seeking empirical evidence of bargaining as a problem-solving strategy. A useful piece, but there is some difficulty with the authors' recommendation that negotiators explicitly identify what has been gained; this might exacerbate conflict and raise new problems.

Schelling, Thomas C. "Bargaining, Communication, and Limited War." *Journal of Conflict Resolution* 1 (1957):19-36. **Organizational conflict, Analytical methods.**

Old but good. This is one of the best statements on implicit/explicit bargaining and communication to reach "limited" agreement. The application to strategic conflict situations does not diminish the general utility of the argument.

――――. "The Strategy of Conflict Prospectus for a Reorientation of Game Theory." *Journal of Conflict Resolution* 2 (1958):203-64. **Organizational conflict, Analytical methods.**

A valuable, well-written primer on game theory and its application to bargaining and negotiation. Although done as part of the "cold-war" studies, this article has useful information on tactics that could be applied to any conflict situation.

Thoenig, J. C. "The Organization and Its Environment: An Approach to the Problems of Public Administration." *Management International Re-*

view 11 (1970):5-14. **Decision models, Management in public organizations.**

A case study of reform where bargaining evolved as the decision mode. A good political interpretation of "resistance to change."

Wall, James A., Jr. "Managing Negotiators." *Business Horizons* 18 (February 1975):41-44. **Managerial functions, Organizational goals and objectives.**

A short discussion of managing negotiations and negotiators. Lightweight, but potentially useful.

Ways, Max. "The Virtues, Dangers, and Limits of Negotiation." *Fortune* (15 January 1979), pp. 86-90. **Organizational conflict.**

A sensible, short statement on bargaining. There is no detailed analysis, but it is still worthwhile.

DECISION ANALYSIS

Bell, Peter. "How to Cope with Uncertainty." *Management Today* (UK) (April 1978), p. 66. **Organizational learning, Risk and uncertainty.**

A good, sensible statement on uncertainty and decisionmaking in organizations. **Recommended.**

Brightman, Harvey, and Nobel, Carl. "On the Ineffective Education of Decision Scientists." *Decision Sciences* 10 (1979):151-57. **Operations research and management science, Analytical methods.**

A critique of the rules and practices of decision science that put potential clients at a disadvantage.

Eden, Colin, and Harris, John. *Management Decision and Decision Analysis.* New York: John Wiley, 1975. **Decision theory, Decision models.**

An excellent book that examines various models of decisionmaking and the implications for management. There is a particularly good section on computer decision models and management information systems.

Forst, Brian E. "Decision Analysis and Medical Malpractice." *Operations Research* 22 (January-February 1974):1-12. **Operations research and management science.**

An example of methodological overstatement, with lots of jargon and technique and little analysis of the problem.

Horowitz, Dan. "Flexible Responsiveness and Military Strategy: The Case of the Israeli Army." *Policy Sciences* 1 (Summer 1970):191-205. **Organizational structure, Risk and uncertainty.**

This excellent case study illustrates how even supposedly tight control organizations can respond to high risk situations without losing organizational integrity.

Jones, David P.; Schipper, Lowell M.; and Holzworth, James R. "Effects of Amount of Information on Decision Strategies." *Journal of General Psychology* 98 (1978):281-94. **Decision theory, Information processing.**

A discussion of the psychological dimensions of information overload and the implications for decisionmaking strategies. This is a narrow but interesting study.

Kernan, Jerome B., and Haines, George H., Jr. "Environmental Search: An Info-Theoretic Approach." *Decision Sciences* 2 (April 1971):161-71. **Information processing, Information management.**

A technical, academic paper that reaches some interesting conclusions about information search limitations. Some data are presented to counter the "more is better" syndrome.

Longbottom, David, and Wade, Geoff. "An Investigation into the Application of Decision Analysis in United Kingdom Companies." *Omega* 1 (1973):207-15. **Decision theory, Risk and uncertainty.**

An excellent study of the use of decision analysis. The findings independently corroborate David Conrath's (1973) on the non-use of probability distribution, for example. **Recommended.**

Mintzberg, Henry. "Research on Strategy-Making." *Academy of Management Proceedings* 32 (1972):90-94. **Policy analysis, Organization and management theory.**

A preliminary research report with no startling conclusions, but some interesting hints on how strategy is developed.

Moore, P. G., and Thomas, H. "Measurement Problems in Decision Analysis." *Journal of Management Studies* 10 (May 1973):168-93. **Planning, Risk and uncertainty.**

A formal presentation of mainstream decision theory. This is interesting in that there is no mention of error correction.

Raiffa, Howard. *Decision Analysis: Introductory Lectures on Choices Under Uncertainty*. Reading, Mass.: Addison-Wesley, 1968. **Risk and uncertainty, Decision theory.**

Raiffa's ideas have been getting some popular attention. This is a good primer.

Richards, Max D. "An Exploratory Study of Strategic Failure." *Academy of Management Proceedings* 33 (1973):40-46. **Evaluation, Organizational effectiveness.**

An excellent study of organizational failure. Unfortunately, the author does not include any successes with which to compare the failures.

Rowe, Alan J. "The Myth of the Rational Decision Maker." *International Management* 29 (August 1974):38-40. **Rationality, Decisionmaking.**

Explains why formal rationality, though perhaps impossible, is nonetheless desirable. Why?

Spekman, Robert E., and Stern, Louis W. "Environmental Uncertainty and Buying Group Structure: An Empirical Investigation." *Journal of Marketing* 43 (Spring 1979):54-64. **Risk and uncertainty, Organizational structure.**

A good analysis of the effect of uncertainty on organizations. As uncertainty increases, the buyer's participation, power, and influence in buying decisions increases.

Thornton, Fred A. "Incremental Analysis Under Conditions of Uncertainty." *Managerial Planning* 26 (May-June 1978):27-31. **Decision theory, Risk and uncertainty.**

A simplistic though pleasant presentation of Decision Theory Analysis (DTA). Not much help except in economically simple situations.

Vroom, Victor H. "A New Look at Managerial Decision Making." *Organizational Dynamics* 1 (Spring 1973):66-80. **Decision models, Decision theory.**

A useful examination of the situation-dependent character of managerial decisionmaking.

DECISION MODELS

Diesing, Paul. *Reason in Society*. Urbana: University of Illinois Press, 1962. **Risk and uncertainty, Rationality.**

The author's dense, convoluted argument makes for difficult reading, but this is a good exposition on decisionmaking. Diesing discusses the various forms of rationality and their relation to risk, uncertainty, and managing organized enterprises.

Hocking, Ralph T., and Hocking, Joan M. "The Evolution of Decision Systems." *MSU Business Topics* 24 (Summer 1976):55-59. **Decision theory, Decision analysis.**

A gross misunderstanding of scientific method leads the authors into erroneous assertions, though the critique of linear decisionmaking is well-founded.

Martin, Merle P. "Decision Making: The Payoff Matrix." *Journal of Systems Management* 30 (January 1979):15-18. **Decisionmaking, Analytical methods.**

Sheer gibberish. If you know what needs to go in the matrix, you don't need the technique.

Pollay, Richard W. "Only the Naive Are Transitive Decision Makers." *Journal of Business Administration* 2 (Fall 1970):3-8. **Decision analysis, Management policy, strategy, and style.**

A critique of the transitive decision models using individual decisionmaking as an illustration.

Whybark, D. Clay. "Comparing an Adaptive Decision Model and Human Decisions." *Academy of Management Journal* 16 (December 1973):700-703. **Decision analysis, Organizational learning.**

A straightforward research report on a decision model and actual performance.

DECISION THEORY

Alexander, Ernest R. "The Limits of Uncertainty: A Note." *Theory and Decision* 6 (1975):363-70. **Risk and uncertainty, Organization and management theory.**

An academic but very interesting discussion of objective and subjective uncertainty and decisionmaking.

Braybrooke, David, and Lindblom, Charles E. *A Strategy of Decision: Policy Evaluation as a Social Process.* New York: Free Press, 1970. **Policy analysis, Incrementalism.**

An outstanding book that provides a systematic comparison of the formally rational "synoptic" decision model and the actual decisionmaking process in large organizations. This is the best statement on the advantages and disadvantages of various approaches to policy and decision analysis. **Recommended.**

Cunningham, A. A., and Turner, I. B. "Decision Analysis for Job Shop Scheduling." *Omega* 1 (1973):733-46. **Decisionmaking, Risk and uncertainty.**

An excellent article that focuses on heuristic vs. optimal decision rules. Consideration of alternatives is handled as a limiting rather than as a general factor.

Delbecq, André L. "Contextual Variables Affecting Decision Making in Program Planning." *Decision Sciences* 5 (October 1974):726-42. **Organizational growth and change, Planning.**

A theoretical essay of some academic interest but of little use to managers unless they are particularly concerned with a minor academic activity.

Kassouf, Sheen. *Normative Decision Making.* Englewood Cliffs, N.J.: Prentice-Hall, 1970. **Decision analysis, Decisionmaking.**

An excellent explanation of the various threads of decision theory. Kassouf makes a very difficult subject accessible, if not completely understandable.

Landau, Martin. "Decision Theory and Comparative Public Administration." *Comparative Political Studies* 1 (July 1968):175-95. **Organization and management theory, Developing countries.**

A useful exposition on decision systems as a basis for comparing management and administration. **Recommended.**

Tuggle, Francis D. "Decision Making Under Uncertainty: Empirical Tests of Normative Theory." *Journal of Business Administration* 4 (Fall 1972):2-9. **Decisionmaking, Risk and uncertainty.**

A useless research exercise, since the problem examined is not clear.

DECISIONMAKING

Allison, Graham T. *Essence of Decision.* Boston: Little, Brown, 1971. **Organization and management theory, Policy analysis.**

A well-known framework of political/bureaucratic decisionmaking. The process is modeled on events during the Cuban Missile Crisis of 1962. A fascinating study, if oversimplified.

Assmus, Gert. "Evaluating Changes in the Marketing Information System." *European Journal of Marketing* 11 (1977):272-80. **Decision analysis, Management information systems.**

A lot of words, but not much useful information. Many formalisms on what is "desired" from an MIS but little on how to realize expectations.

Becker, Selwyn W.; Ronen, Joshua; and Sorter, George H. "Opportunity Costs: An Experimental Approach." *Journal of Accounting Research* 12 (Autumn 1974):317-29. **Accounting, Cost-benefit analysis.**

An interesting study of the effect formal accounting procedures have on decisionmakers' consideration of opportunity costs. This is an enlightening and useful discussion of intuitive and formal decision processes.

Blakemore, Colin. "The Unsolved Marvel of Memory." *New York Times Magazine* (6 February 1977), pp. 42-46. **Problem solving, Risk and uncertainty.**

An interesting discussion of human memory and implications for man-computer interaction. Blakemore makes some sensible comments on information overload.

Duncan, Robert B. "Characteristics of Organizational Environments and Perceived Environmental Uncertainty." *Administrative Science Quarterly* 17 (September 1972):313-27. **Decision analysis, Risk and uncertainty.**

A rather confusing attempt to refine definitions of environment, uncertainty, and decision.

Eccles, A. J., and Wood, D. "How Do Managers Decide?" *Journal of Management Studies* 9 (October 1972):291-302. **Managerial functions, Comparative management.**

An interesting study that compares the differences between experienced and inexperienced managers in different decisionmaking situations.

Ford, Charles H. "Time to Redesign the Decision-Making Process." *Management Review* 67 (July 1978):50-53. **Decision analysis, Managerial functions.**

A simplistic call to shift organizations into "high gear" and to get middle management more involved in decisionmaking.

Gabor, P. "Management Theory and Rational Decision Making." *Management Decision* 14 (1976):274-81. **Analytical methods, Rationality.**

A thoughtful article on the fact/value elements of decisionmaking. The argument is not well-developed and appears trivial, but it is not. This article is interesting because there are so few like it.

Harrison, F. L. "Decision-Making in Conditions of Extreme Uncertainty." *Journal of Management Studies* 14 (May 1977):169-78. **Analytical methods, Decision analysis.**

An interesting essay with some information on how probability estimates are juggled to justify a decision. The author's suggested alternative seems just as liable to be tinkered with.

Hesse, Rick, and Altman, Steve. "Star Trek: An Optimum Decision Making Model." *Interfaces* 6 (May 1976):60-62. **Decision models, Operations research and management science.**

Lightweight but sensible and illustrative, this is a good "pop" model to be passed around.

Horowitz, Ira. *Decision Making and the Theory of the Firm.* New York: Holt, Rinehart, and Winston, 1970. **Economic analysis, Organization and management theory.**

A literate and useful extension of the theory of the firm into decisionmaking strategies. Some technical economic language, but otherwise clear.

Isaack, Thomas S. "Intuition: An Ignored Dimension of Management." *Academy of Management Review* 3 (October 1978):917-21. **Organization and management theory, Rationality.**

A short look at intuition in management decisionmaking. There is not enough here to be of much use, but it is worth reading because the subject has been neglected in the literature.

Kaufman, Carolyn Chambers, and McKeon, Joseph M. "Accounting for the Uncertain You." *Journal of Systems Management* 29 (February 1978):33-37. **Analytical methods.**

An oversimplified decision "tool" of doubtful utility.

Kaufman, Felix. "Decision Making: Eastern and Western Style." *Business Horizons* 13 (December 1970):81-86. **Comparative management, Planning.**

A discussion of Japanese consensual decision style. It is a difficult method to install out of cultural context, but the author suggests a synthesis.

Leemans, A. F. "The Spatial Hierarchy of Decision Making." *Development and Change* 1 (1969-70):14-29. **Policy analysis, Developing countries.**

Objectives, space, and decisions. It is hard to tell what Leemans's message is.

Love, Sidney F. "Group Decisions Without Conflict; Divided Is Undecided." *CA Magazine* 109 (August 1976):52-55. **Decision models.**

A short outline of a group decisionmaking process. Love presents a quick consensus method, provided all agree to participate.

March, James G. "The 1978 Nobel Prize in Economics." *Science* 202 (24 November 1978):858-61. **Organization and management theory, Decision analysis.**

A tribute to Herbert Simon and his Nobel Prize, this is a short review of Simon's work and his contributions to our understanding of organizations and decisionmaking.

Marks, Barry A. "Decision Under Uncertainty: A Poet's View." *Business Horizons* 14 (February 1971):57-61. **Risk and uncertainty.**

A nice little diversion, though not to be taken lightly. Marks presents an interesting perspective on decisionmaking, rationality, and accountability.

Marney, Milton. "Institutional Self-Organization." *Policy Sciences* 2 (1971):117-42. **Management control, Organizational structure.**

An example of how jargon, fuzzy reasoning, and convoluted language combine to say nothing useful to anyone.

May, Andrew. "Charting the Pros and Cons." *Industrial Management* (December 1976), pp. 17-19. **Participative management.**

A trivial and shallow exercise that "charts" a group approach to relatively straightforward decisionmaking circumstances.

Moore, P. G. "Technique vs. Judgment in Decision Making." *Organizational Dynamics* 2 (Autumn 1973):69-80. **Management control, Management education and training.**

A sensible analysis of intuitive decisionmaking and its relationship to formal techniques. Moore overstates the use of probability in dealing with uncertainty. He also perpetuates the PERT/Polaris myth.

Morrisey, George L. "The Decision Matrix." *Personnel Administrator* 21 (September 1976):37-39. **Analytical methods, Management by objectives.**

Sheer nonsense. The matrix contributes nothing to understanding or making decisions.

Moses, Michael A. "Implementation of Analytical Planning Systems." *Management Science* 21 (June 1975):1133-43. **Strategic planning, Analytical methods.**

The author outlines a system to enhance efficiency in decisionmaking by assisting in selecting and implementing "optimal" policies. We still don't know how this is done.

Nolan, Terry J., and Banda, A. Frederic. "An Empirical Study of the Capital Investment Decision Making Process in Selected Ohio Companies in 1971, Part I." *Akron Business and Economic Review* 3 (Spring 1972):10-16. "Part II." 3 (Summer 1972):12-19. **Planning, Risk and uncertainty.**

An interesting examination of factors in capital investment decisions. It seems that payback is preferred to more sophisticated methods.

Nutt, Paul C. "Models for Decision Making in Organizations and Some Contextual Variables Which Stipulate Optimal Use." *Academy of Management Review* 1 (April 1976):84-98. **Decision models, Organization and management theory.**

An effort to expand decision models. It does so, but it doesn't add much to what is already available.

Olson, Philip D. "Notes: Decision Making—Type I and Type II Error

Analysis." *California Management Review* 20 (Fall 1977):81-83. **Analytical methods, Operations research and management science.**

A short discussion of error analysis. The author's Type I and Type II distinction does not follow the technical statistical analogy.

Phelps, Ruth H., and Shanteau, James. "Livestock Judges: How Much Information Can an Expert Use?" *Organizational Behavior and Human Performance* 21 (1978):209-19. **Information management, Information processing.**

Interesting only because of the discussion of the psychological limits of information that even experts can use.

Roach, John M. "Decision Making Is a 'Satisficing' Experience." *Management Review* 68 (January 1979):8-17. **Management theory, Economic analysis.**

An update on Herbert Simon's thinking in an interview prompted by his 1978 Nobel Prize in economics.

Roberts, Ralph M., and Hanline, Manning H. "Maximizing Executive Effectiveness: Deciding About What to Decide." *Management Review* 20 (January 1976):22-25. **Organization and management theory, Management control.**

A trite, cliché-ridden misunderstanding of management decision.

Rowan, Roy. "Those Business Hunches Are More Than Blind Faith." *Fortune* 99 (23 April 1979):110-14. **Managerial functions.**

Short and sensible. Rowan presents some very interesting information, though no analysis.

Shuler, Cyril O. "How Good Are Decision Makers?" *Business Horizons* 18 (April 1975):89-93. **Organizational behavior, Management effectiveness.**

A modest effort at assessing managerial decisions. The author uses the analogy of a baseball player's batting average to appraise managerial decisionmaking.

Shumway, C. R. et al. "Diffuse Decision-Making in Hierarchical Organizations: An Empirical Examination." *Management Science* 21 (February 1975):697-707. **Hierarchy, Organization and management theory.**

A study of how decisions are spread over a system rather than localized in terms of managers controlling, organizing, planning, etc.

Simon, Herbert. "The Unconventional Economic Man." *International Management* 34 (April 1979):26-29. **Rationality, Organization and management theory.**

A short talk with Herbert Simon, following his acceptance of the Nobel Prize in economics.

Taylor, Ronald N. "Concepts, Theory and Techniques: Psychological Determinants of Bounded Rationality—Implications for Decision Making Strategies." *Decision Sciences* 6 (July 1975):409-29. **Information processing, Rationality.**

An academic exercise, of no immediate use to managers and with little new for the researcher.

van de Ven, Andrew H. "A Panel Study on the Effects of Task Uncertainty, Interdependence, and Size on Unit Decision Making." *Organization and Administrative Sciences* 8 (Summer-Fall 1977):237-53. **Decentralization, Organizational design.**

A theoretical piece with implications for organizational design and the installation of control systems. This is difficult reading, but the findings may be worth the effort.

Welsch, Lawrence A., and Cyert, Richard M., eds. *Management Decision Making*. Baltimore: Penguin, 1971. **Managerial functions, Organization and management theory.**

An excellent collection. Penguin has done us a great service by publishing these books of readings. This one provides some of the best articles on the subject in a convenient, affordable form. **Recommended.**

Yankelovich, Daniel. "Managing in an Age of Anxiety." *Industry Week* 195 (24 October 1977):52. **Risk and uncertainty, Control systems and techniques.**

A meandering discussion with no clear conclusion.

INCREMENTALISM

Lasserre, Ph. "Planning Through Incrementalism." *Socio-Economic Planning Sciences* 8 (1974):129-34. **Planning, Organization and management theory.**

An unsuccessful attempt to reconcile incrementalism and rational comprehensive planning.

Lindblom, Charles E. "The Science of 'Muddling Through'." *Public Administration Review* 19 (Spring 1959):79-88. **Decisionmaking, Organization and management theory.**

A classic that must be read to be at all familiar with the field. **Recommended.**

———. "Still Muddling, Not Yet Through." *Public Administration Review*

39 (November-December 1979):517-26. **Decisionmaking, Organization and management theory.**

An update of the original, on the 20th anniversary of publication. The ideas have not dimmed with time. Still brilliant, still insightful, and probably never through. **Recommended.**

Quinn, James Brian. "Strategic Change: 'Logical Incrementalism'." *Sloan Management Review* 20 (Fall 1978):7-21. **Organizational growth and change, Organization and management theory, Decisionmaking.**

An excellent piece on the power and logic of incremental change. **Highly recommended.**

PROBLEM SOLVING

Aronofsky, Julius S., ed. *Progress in Operations Research.* Vol. 3: *Relationship Between Operations Research and the Computer.* New York: John Wiley, 1969. **Operations research and management science, Computer services.**

It is a cliché to describe an essay collection as "uneven," yet most are. This one is useful primarily because of Allen Newell's contribution on ill-structured problems.

Brightman, Harvey J. "Concepts, Theories and Techniques: Differences in Ill-Structured Problem Solving Along the Organizational Hierarchy." *Decision Sciences* 9 (January 1978):1-18. **Organizational structure, Hierarchy.**

An intelligent piece that deserves more attention than it is likely to receive. "The case of the worn-out plates" is a perfect illustration of problems managers must deal with. **Highly recommended.**

Edwards, Morris O. "Creativity Solves Management Problems." *Management Notes* 20 (January 1976):1-7. **Organizational learning, Analytical methods.**

Another gimmick. This one is called Creative Problem Solving (CPS) and can be taught by the author's firm. A long commercial.

Mitroff, Ian I., and Emshoff, James R. "On Strategic Assumption-Making: A Dialectical Approach to Policy Planning." *Academy of Management Review* 4 (1979):1-12. **Planning, Analytical methods.**

Another attempt to come up with a well-structured technique to deal with ill-structured problems. There is no harm in trying.

Mosher, Charles D. "How to Identify Management Problems." *GAO Review* (Fall 1973), pp. 8-16. **Management effectiveness, Organizational learning.**

Another useless process model for problem identification.

Platt, John R. "Strong Inference." *Science* 146 (16 October 1964):347-53. **Organization and management theory, Decision theory.**

A brilliant essay on science and popular misconceptions of what it is and is not. Platt makes some very telling statements on the acceptance of theories that are incapable of disproof.

Pounds, William F. "The Scheduling Environment." In *Industrial Scheduling,* edited by John F. Muth and Gerald L. Thompson. Englewood Cliffs, N.J.: Prentice-Hall, 1963, pp. 5-12. **Operations research and management science, Analytical methods.**

The book is technical and esoteric, but Pounds's essay is sensible and pragmatic. Tools, techniques, or solutions, Pounds argues, have meaning only when agreement on what constitutes a problem has been reached.

————. "The Process of Problem Finding." *Industrial Management Review* 11 (Fall 1969):1-19. **Organization and management theory, Decision models.**

A good outline of the models that influence problem definition, with scant consideration of the source of the problem.

Sanderson, Mike. "Successful Problem Finding." *Journal of Systems Management* 25 (October 1974):16-21. **Systems analysis.**

A rare discussion of problem diagnosis, though not all that well done. The author discusses premature problem structuring by using available solutions (solving the wrong problem).

Simon, Herbert A. "The Structure of Ill-Structured Problems." *Artificial Intelligence* 4 (Winter 1973):181-201. **Decisionmaking, Organization and management theory.**

An interesting article by one of the pioneers in pragmatic organization theory. **Highly recommended.**

Strauch, Ralph E. "'Squishy' Problems and Quantitative Methods." *Policy Sciences* 6 (1975):175-84. **Analytical methods, Modeling and simulation.**

A short examination of the limitations of quantitative methods in solving problems.

Swinth, Robert L. "Organizational Joint Problem-Solving." *Management Science* 18 (October 1971):B68-79. **Planning, Organizational learning.**

A bit muddled, but an interesting experiment comparing organizational servo-mechanisms and a problem-solving approach.

Taylor, Ronald N. "Nature of Problem Ill-Structuredness: Implications for Problem Formulation and Solutions." *Decision Sciences* 5 (October 1974):632-43. **Decisionmaking, Rationality.**

A clear statement, with an explanation of various problem-solving strategies and circumstances.

Tuggle, Francis D.; Swinth, Robert L.; and Fegan, Charles R. "Coping with Ill-Defined Decisions and Problems." *Journal of Business Administration* 6 (Spring 1975):1-12. **Decision theory, Decisionmaking.**

A short article that offers a few decision rules for ill-structured problems.

RATIONALITY

Regan, D. E. "Rationality in Policymaking: Two Concepts Not One." *Long Range Planning* 11 (October 1978):83-88. **Decisionmaking, Policymaking.**

An examination of various definitions and types of rationality in decisionmaking and policymaking. A nice primer, but not much more.

Wagner, John A., III. "The Organizational Double Bind: Toward an Understanding of Rationality and Its Complement." *Academy of Management Review* 3 (October 1978):786-95. **Organization and management theory, Organizational behavior.**

A formal discussion with some interesting observations.

RISK AND UNCERTAINTY

Atherton, Judith. "Measures of Risk and Risk Aversion." *Managerial Finance* 4 (1978):252-68. **Decisionmaking, Decision analysis.**

A technical examination of decisionmaking in calculable risk domains. Nothing new, but an interesting piece.

Carter, E. Eugene. "What Are the Risks in Risk Analysis?" *Harvard Business Review* 50 (July-August 1972):72-82. **Organizational design, Operations research and management science.**

An idiosyncratic, anecdotal exhortation for "risk analysis." Whatever it is, it is good according to the author, who tells us how to avoid "troublespots."

Churchman, C. West. "Preparation for Uncertainty." *Organizational Dynamics* 1 (Summer 1972):12-20. **Management education and training, Operations research and management science.**

One of his better short pieces, there are some solid thoughts here. See especially the "Errors of Preparation" section. **Recommended.**

Downey, H. Kirk, and Slocum, John W. "Uncertainty: Measures, Research, and Sources of Variation." *Academy of Management Journal* 18 (September 1975):562-78. **Organization and management theory, Organizational psychology.**

An examination of the psychological dimensions of organizational and environmental uncertainty. Primarily a research agenda.

Goff, Harrison H. "Risk Management: Training Ground for the Top." *Financial Executive* 47 (February 1979):22-27. **Management education and training, Manager and controller roles.**

A formal discussion of financial risk assessment. The author sees risk management as a training ground for future senior managers. But risk equals insurance assessment.

Hardy, Charles O. *Risk and Risk-Bearing*. Chicago: University of Chicago Press, 1923. **Managerial functions, Organization and management theory.**

A classic statement on the pervasive organizational condition. Hardy's explanation of the relation of risk to management has not been (and probably cannot be) improved. **Recommended.**

Huff, Anne S. "Consensual Uncertainty." *Academy of Management Review* 3 (July 1978):651-55. **Decision analysis, Organizational learning.**

An interesting conceptual exploration of uncertainty and its effect on organizational decisionmaking. Original and thought provoking.

Kania, John J., and McKean, John R. "Decision-Making in the Extensive Firm." *Nebraska Journal of Economics and Business* 18 (Winter 1979):25-42. **Organization and management theory, Management policy, strategy, and style, Decisionmaking.**

An examination of the influence of profit-making and managerial decisionmaking. An interesting issue, but not a very good article.

Knight, Frank H. *Risk, Uncertainty and Profit*. Boston: Houghton Mifflin, 1921. Reprint. Chicago: University of Chicago Press, 1971. **Organization and management theory, Economic analysis.**

A classic essay on the concepts of risk and uncertainty in organizations. Knight's book is still the best work on the subject. **Highly recommended.**

Schmidt, Stuart M., and Cummings, Larry L. "Organizational Environment, Differentiation and Perceived Environmental Uncertainty." *Decision Sciences* 7 (July 1976):447-67. **Decisionmaking, Organizational effectiveness.**

A technical examination, this article tries to add an empirical dimension to perceived environmental uncertainty (PEU), organizational structure, and objective uncertainty. A difficult task, not accomplished.

Schwarz, William L. K. "Risk or Uncertainty? The Corporate Decision-Maker's Dilemma." *Finance* 96 (March 1978):17-20. **Decisionmaking, Organization and management theory.**

A short but intelligent discussion of risk, uncertainty, and belief in decisionmaking.

Spulber, Nicolas, and Horowitz, Ira. *Quantitative Economic Policy and Planning.* New York: W. W. Norton, 1976. **Economic analysis, Decision theory.**

A useful book that deserves wider attention. The authors' discussion of economic and organizational "as if" formulations is particularly well done. **Recommended.**

Trinkl, Frank H. "Resource Allocation Under Uncertainty." *Policy Sciences* 6 (March 1975):29-40. **Decisionmaking, Policy analysis.**

A highly unrealistic formal restructuring of uncertainty through stipulation and assumption.

Developing Countries

DEVELOPMENT PLANNING

Ackoff, Russell L. "National Development Planning Revisited." *Operations Research* 25 (March-April 1977):207-18. **Economic development, Organizational design.**

A plea for an "idealized design" approach to development planning. This is not quite as thoughtful and useful as most of Ackoff's work.

Caiden, Naomi, and Wildavsky, Aaron. *Planning and Budgeting in Poor Countries.* New York: John Wiley, 1974. **Budgeting, Policy analysis.**

The first systematic effort to empirically investigate planning and budgeting in developing countries. This is a fine work that must be considered when appraising the contribution of formal planning theory in resource-short economies. **Recommended.**

Dror, Yehezkel. *Systems Analysis for Development Decisions: Applicability, Feasibility, Effectiveness and Efficiency.* P-4159. Santa Monica, Calif.: RAND Corporation, August 1969. **Systems analysis.**

A good essay that outlines when systems analysis can be usefully applied in development.

Enthoven, Adolf J. H. "The Scope for Accountancy Planning in Developing Countries." *Accounting and Business Research* 6 (Spring 1976):135-39. **Accounting, Management in developing countries.**

A guide to improving accountancy practices and education in LDCs.

Goodman, Seymour S. "The Paradox of Development Planning." *Omega* 2 (1974):625-34. **Planning, Risk and uncertainty.**

An academic piece on the critical uncertainties of development planning.

Gross, Bertram M. "Management Strategy for Economic and Social Development: Part I." *Policy Sciences* 2 (1971):339-71. "Part II." 3 (1972):1-25. **Economic development, Management in public organizations.**

This piece is overlong (it could have easily been compressed into a single article), but there are some valuable suggestions in all those words. Gross is a fine scholar with an excellent grasp of the problems facing developing countries.

————. "Destructive Decision-Making in Developing Countries." *Policy Sciences* 5 (1974):213-36. **Decisionmaking.**

An examination/critique of a number of fallacies in LDC decisionmaking premises. No new ground is broken, but this is a good overview.

Lee, Hahn-Been. "Developmentalist Time and Leadership in Developing Countries." CAG Occasional Papers. Comparative Administrative Group, American Society for Public Administration, 1965. **Comparative management.**

A good example of the thinking and recommendations prevalent among academics in the sixties.

Milne, R. S. "Decision-Making in Developing Countries." *Journal of Comparative Administration* 3 (February 1972):387-404. **Decisionmaking.**

An intelligent appraisal of incremental vs. radical change decisionmaking strategies in developing countries.

Packard, Philip C., and Wit, Daniel. "Government and the Implementation of Economic Plans in New and Emerging States." *Development and Change* 1 (1969-70):1-13. **Economic development.**

Nothing new. Another statement on central planning for development.

Pyatt, Graham, and Thorbecke, Erik. *Planning Techniques for a Better Future*. Geneva: International Labour Organization, 1976. **Economic planning, Policy analysis.**

Another attempt at social accounting. The authors offer an economic planning model to increase growth and recommend that countries redistribute wealth to reduce poverty. Flawed in economic assumptions vs. political possibilities.

Raghavulu, C. V. "Administrative Reform: A Study of an Intensive Agricultural Programme in India." *Journal of Administration Overseas* 17 (July 1978):191-200. **Management in developing countries, Administrative reform.**

An excellent capsule case of administrative reform in India. This is a good examination of outside intervention in a well-developed bureaucratic structure and the results for institutions and development.

Rondinelli, Dennis A. "Preparing and Analyzing Case Studies in Development Project Management." *Technos* 5 (April-June 1976):29-40. **Project management.**

A "how-to" outline for development project design and management. Actual utility is an empirical question, and is as yet unanswered.

———. "Planning Development Projects: Lessons from Developing Countries." *Long Range Planning* 12 (June 1979):48-56. **Project management.**

The author has written extensively on the subject. Unfortunately, he keeps saying the same thing: Project planning requires a broad perspective.

———, and Palia, Aspy P., eds. *Project Planning and Implementation in Developing Countries*. Honolulu: Technology and Development Institute, The East-West Center, 1976. **Project management, Policy analysis.**

The usual mixed bag of essays on development project design and implementation. This is not a significant contribution to the already voluminous literature, but there are some useful suggestions.

Rothwell, Kenneth J., ed. *Administrative Issues in Developing Economies*. Lexington, Mass.: D. C. Heath, 1972. **Administrative reform, Management in public organizations.**

There are some interesting essays (e.g., Ida Hoos, W. J. Siffin, and F. W. Riggs) in this otherwise lackluster collection. In comparing these edited sets, it is most interesting to note how little progress is made on the "issues."

van Dam, André. "Corporate Planning for Asia, Latin America and Africa." *Long Range Planning* 5 (December 1972):2-8. **Planning, Management policy, strategy, and style.**

Discussion of the planner-as-hero, the answer to all problems in the Third World. This is interesting because of the overstatement of the planner's role in influencing the future.

Wildavksy, Aaron. "Why Planning Fails in Nepal." *Administrative Science Quarterly* 17 (December 1972):508-28. **Economic development.**

An astute, empirical look at development planning in Nepal. There are some lessons here for all planners, particularly those in LDCs.

ECONOMIC DEVELOPMENT

Baum, Warren C. "The World Bank Project Cycle." *Finance and Development* 15 (December 1978):10-17. **Foreign aid, Project management.**

A detailed outline of the World Bank's project process, from identification through implementation and evaluation. This is a useful update of Baum's 1970 article from the same journal.

Caplan, Basil. "Kenya's Pragmatism Pays Off." *The Banker* 129 (March 1979):29-34. **Policy analysis.**

An economic and financial appraisal of Kenya's past and future. This is a good, short profile of successful African capitalism and pluralist democracy.

Dunn, Edgar S., Jr. *Economic and Social Development.* Baltimore: The Johns Hopkins University Press, 1971. **Economic planning, Policy analysis.**

This book has not received the attention it deserves. It is a noteworthy attempt at modeling organizational and social learning as an evolutionary process.

Hazledine, Tim, and Moreland, R. Scott. "Population and Economic Growth: A World Cross-Section Study." *Review of Economics and Statistics* 59 (August 1977):253-63. **Modeling and simulation.**

A model of demographic and economic influences on the world. OK, if you believe in this sort of thing.

Hirschman, Albert O. "Policymaking and Policy Analysis in Latin America: A Return Journey." *Policy Sciences* 6 (1975):385-402. **Policymaking, Policy analysis.**

An update on some of the author's earlier work. **Recommended.**

Kee, Woo Sik. "Fiscal Decentralization and Economic Development." *Public Finance Quarterly* 5 (January 1977):79-97. **Decentralization.**

A formal examination of the effect of fiscal decentralization on 64 selected countries (developed and developing).

Negandhi, Anant R. *Management and Economic Development: The Case of Taiwan.* The Hague: Martinus Nijhoff, 1973. **Comparative management.**

An analysis of the role of management expertise in economic development. Taiwan is a model of an economic success story that is often suggested to LDCs. There are some lessons here.

Oh, Tai K. "Theory Y in the People's Republic of China." *California Management Review* 19 (Winter 1976):77-84. **Comparative management, Organization and management theory.**

An optimistic appraisal of the PRC's industrial progress, with major attribution to the Chinese application of principles similar to McGregor's Theory Y. I don't think the author understands McGregor's ideas.

Patton, Carl Vernon. "Budgeting Under Crisis: The Confederacy as a Poor Country." *Administrative Science Quarterly* 20 (September 1975):355-70. **Budgeting.**

An interesting exercise in testing hypotheses on budgeting behavior in uncertain resource-short environments. The Confederacy did indeed show some of the same budget patterns as modern LDCs.

Rondinelli, Dennis A. "Project Identification in Economic Development." *Journal of World Trade Law* 10 (1976):215-51. **Project management.**

An examination of various foreign assistance agencies' project identification processes.

Rose, Sanford. "Third World 'Commodity Power' Is a Costly Illusion." *Fortune* 94 (November 1976):147. **Organizational objectives, Economic analysis.**

A short statement on one of the principal elements of the North-South dialogue (or struggle) that is so much a part of governmental policy.

Schnarch, Alexander. "R&D Policy in China After the Cultural Revolution." *Research Management* 19 (January 1976):28-32. **Research and development.**

A quick look at R&D in the People's Republic of China. It may be a bit dated, but this article can be used to see just how disruptive the Cultural Revolution was.

Systems Analysis and Operations Research: A Tool for Policy and Program Planning for Developing Countries. Report of an Ad Hoc Panel of the Board on Science and Technology for International Development, Commission on International Relations. Washington, D.C.: National Aeronautics and Space Administration, 1976. **Systems analysis, Operations research and management science.**

Economic development, systems analysis, and operations research. This short report views SA/OR as the answer to all LDC problems. There are some caveats, but the tone is generally optimistic and simplistic.

FOREIGN AID

Owens, Edgar, and Shaw, Robert. *Development Reconsidered.* Lexington, Mass.: D. C. Heath, 1972. **Economic development.**

A long, rather tedious exhortation for a "reconsideration" of U.S. foreign assistance policy. The *why* is to help poor people; what is missing is the *how*.

Strachan, Harry W. "Side-Effects of Planning in the Aid Control System."

World Development 6 (1978):467-78. **Economic development, Organizational effectiveness.**

A good analysis of the effect an inappropriate control system had on delivery of U.S. foreign assistance, a notoriously uncertain domain.

Tendler, Judith. *Inside Foreign Aid.* Baltimore: The Johns Hopkins University Press, 1975. **Development planning, Management in developing countries.**

So far the best study of U.S. bilateral foreign assistance programs. Tendler's analysis of the interplay of economics and organizational factors is brilliant. **Highly recommended.**

INDUSTRIAL DEVELOPMENT

Boehm, Barry W., and Dexter, Benton G., Jr. "Some Software Considerations for Developing Countries." *Technos* 4 (January-March 1975):32-43. **Computer services, Training in developing countries.**

A shallow, huckstering piece that presumes a need for computer hardware and presents a planning model for software development.

Brasch, John J. "Sales Forecasting Difficulties in a Developing Country." *Industrial Marketing Management* 7 (October 1978):354-60. **Analytical methods, Planning.**

A study of market forecasting in El Salvador. The author found that techniques and planning do not overcome problems of uncertainty.

Carter, Richard D.; Hamilton, John G.; and Williams, Peter J. "Corporate Planning in Developing Economies." *Long Range Planning* 6 (June 1973):2-5. **Planning, Management in developing countries.**

A "state of the art" piece on corporate planning in developing countries. Since the task is so immense, there is little that is gained from formal exercises like this one.

Dore, R. P. "Late Development—Or Something Else? Industrial Relations in Britain, Japan, Mexico, Sri Lanka, Senegal." Institute of Development Studies, Communication Series no. 61. Sussex, England: University of Sussex, August 1974. **Bargaining and negotiation, Development planning.**

A well-crafted study of employer-employee relations, with a number of interesting findings and suggestions for further research.

Gerstenfeld, Arthur, and Wortzel, Lawrence H. "Strategies for Innovation in Developing Countries." *Sloan Management Review* 19 (Fall 1977): 57-68. **Economic development, Innovation.**

A rather cursory examination of industrial innovation potential in developing countries based on Taiwan data. The results may not be generalizable, but the discussion of demand effects on technological innovations is interesting.

Lebell, Don; Schultz, Konrad; and Weston, Fred J. "Small-Scale Industries and Developing Countries." *California Management Review* 17 (Fall 1974):32-40. **Development planning.**

An ambitious piece that would have LDC entrepreneurs repeat all the mistakes inherent in prescriptions for planning. Misguided advice to be ignored in LDCs and regretted by responsible advisers.

Vertinsky, Ilan. "OR/MS Implementation in Valle, Colombia, S.A.: A Profile of a Developing Region." *Management Science* 18 (February 1972): B314-27. **Operations research and management science, Risk and uncertainty.**

A good case study with some useful observations on the disutility of tight control schemes in conditions of high uncertainty.

Wells, Louis T., Jr. "Negotiating with Third World Governments." *Harvard Business Review* 55 (January-February 1977):72-80. **Bargaining and negotiation, Planning.**

How to handle private investment in developing countries. There is not much detail, but some cautionary notes are worth heeding.

INSTITUTIONAL DEVELOPMENT

Blase, Melvin G. *Institution Building: A Source Book.* Bloomington: PASITAM, Indiana University, 1973. **Organization and management theory.**

A useful annotated survey of the institution building literature. Though not as popular as it was in the sixties, institution building retains some interest for those concerned with encouraging the growth of stable, purposive organizations. This book is a good guide.

Singh, Paul. "Problems of Local Government Reform in a Small State: The Case of Barbados." *Journal of Administration Overseas* 14 (April 1975): 105-12. **Administrative reform, Decentralization.**

A good case study of centralization-decentralization tensions.

MANAGEMENT IN DEVELOPING COUNTRIES

Adamolekun, 'Ladipo. "Accountability and Control Measures in Public Bureaucracies." *International Review of Administrative Sciences* 4 (1974):307-21. **Bureaucracy, Control systems and techniques.**

An analysis of politics, administration, and accountability in public agencies in a number of African countries. This is interesting for the views expressed on external influences.

Balogun, M. J. "Typologies of Management Improvement." *International Review of Administrative Sciences* 40 (1974):245-54. **Management education and training, Management in public organizations.**

Essentially a literature review, this is nevertheless an excellent example of the influence industrialized countries have on management approaches in developing countries.

Black, T. R. L., and Farley, John U. "The Application of Market Research in Contraceptive Social Marketing in a Rural Area of Kenya." *Journal of the Market Research Society* 21 (January 1979):30-43. **Policy analysis.**

Loaded with jargon, but an interesting empirical study. This article is useful in judging the utility of market research advertising in social welfare programs.

Crosby, John. "Personnel Management in a Developing Country." *Personnel Management* 8 (September 1976):19-23. **Personnel management, Manager and controller roles.**

A good survey of developing country problems with a focus on Zambia. Crosby reviews government and business relationships.

Cullinan, Terrence. "Latin American Management Education and Recruitment: An Environmental Perspective." *California Management Review* 12 (Spring 1970):35-43. **Management education and training, Training in developing countries.**

A survey of Latin American management practices and potentials, this article is useful as a guide to influences on management in developing countries.

Damachi, Ukandi G. *Theories of Management and the Executive in the Developing World.* London: Macmillan, 1978. **Comparative management, Organization and management theory.**

The first eight chapters are summaries of trends in organization and management theory. Concluding case studies on the "African style" of management (chapters 9-11) are simplistic, but insightful. Useful in understanding the LDC scholar's view of management.

Flores, Filemon. "The Applicability of American Management Practices to Developing Countries: A Case Study of the Philippines." *Management International Review* 12 (1972):83-89. **Comparative management, Organization and management theory.**

An example of how management principles are *presumed* to work effectively in the U.S. without regard for situational constraints. The principles are then applied to LDC organizations as grading criteria.

Garcia-Zamor, Jean-Claude. "Development Administration in the Commonwealth Caribbean." *International Review of Administrative Sciences* 36 (1970):201-14. **Development planning, Management in public organizations.**

An interesting though dated analysis of public management in the Anglophone Caribbean nations. There are some general insights, but the article is heavily area-specific.

Hardiman, Margaret, and Midgley, James. "Foreign Consultants and Development Projects: The Need for an Alternative Approach." *Journal of Administration Overseas* 17 (October 1978):232-44. **Consultants, Development planning.**

An interesting experiment with foreign consulting services in Sierra Leone. The approach will not work everywhere, but it's worth a look.

Henley, John S. "The Personnel Professionals of Kenya." *Personnel Management* 9 (February 1977):10-14. **Personnel management.**

A summary of the author's research into personnel practices of private firms in Kenya.

Israel, Arturo. "Toward Better Project Implementation." *Finance and Development* 15 (March 1978):27-30. **Project management, Development planning.**

A World Bank view of development project design and implementation.

Lauter, Geza Peter. "Advanced Management Processes in Developing Countries: Planning in Turkey." *California Management Review* 12 (Spring 1970):7-12. **Organization and management theory, Planning.**

A rehash of classical management principles and development planning in Turkey.

————. "Environmental Constraints Impeding Managerial Performance in Developing Countries." *Management International Review* 10 (1970):45-52. **Management models, Organization and management theory.**

The author uses classical management principles as a measure of the application of "advanced management practices" in developing countries—a questionable enterprise since it is doubtful that such practices are used in industrialized countries.

Marston, Ronald C. "Management Expertise: Its Application in Developing Countries." *Personnel Administrator* 23 (August 1978):54-56. **Management effectiveness.**

A preachy piece on multinational corporation managers working in developing countries.

Mohan, Lakshmi, and Bean, Alden S. "Operational Research in India: An Evaluation of the Current State of the Art *vis-à-vis* Potential." *Operational Research Quarterly* 27 (1976):547-65. **Operations research and management science, Comparative management.**

A good review of operations research and management science practices in India, with some interesting observations for application in other developing countries.

Motta, Paulo Roberto. "The Incompatibility of Good Planning and Bad Management: Implementation Problems in Development Administration." Technical Paper Series no. 3. Institute of Latin American Studies, University of Texas at Austin, 1976, pp. 1-28. **Development planning, Management in public organizations.**

A discussion of planning and management issues in developing countries. This is a bit awkward and repetitious at times, but still worth a look.

Muhammad, Faqir. "Use of Modern Management Approaches and Techniques in Public Administration." *International Review of Administrative Sciences* 37 (1971):187-200. **Operations research and management science, Management in public organizations.**

An overview of various approaches and techniques and their applicability and acceptability in developing countries.

Negandhi, Anant R. *Organization Theory in an Open System*. Port Washington, N.Y.: Kennikat Press, 1975. **Comparative management, Organization and management theory.**

A formal appraisal of the transferability of "modern" management techniques to industrial firms in developing countries. The concentration is on formal principles and process.

———, and Reimann, Bernard C. "A Contingency Theory of Organization Re-Examined in the Context of a Developing Country." *Academy of Management Journal* 15 (June 1972):137-46. **Comparative management, Contingency theory.**

A mildly interesting study testing some of the hypotheses of contingency theory in India.

Packard, Philip C. "Management and Control of Parastatal Organizations." *Development and Change* 3 (1971-72):62-76. **Development planning, Industrial development.**

A very good article on a much-neglected subject. This is an analysis of Tanzania's experience with public corporations. Much more work is needed in this area, and this piece is a good beginning. Packard discusses organizational control as a political issue. **Recommended.**

Peterson, R. E., and Seo, K. K. "Public Administration Planning in Developing Countries: A Bayesian Decision Theory Approach." *Policy Sciences* 3 (September 1972):371-78. **Decision theory, Management in public organizations.**

A formalistic exercise that borders on silliness. The utility of the approach is assumed in industrial countries' public agencies and then extended to developing countries.

Pezeshkpur, Changiz. "Challenges to Management in the Arab World." *Business Horizons* 21 (August 1978):47-55. **Comparative management, Managerial functions.**

Management, Islamic fatalism, and Middle Eastern customs are compared with the formally rational approaches considered typical of North American businesses.

Rapoport, Carla. "Why the Spending Stopped in Nigeria." *Fortune* 100 (16 July 1979):146-54.

A quick appraisal of the business and political signs in Nigeria.

Reynolds, John I. "Developing Policy Responses to Cultural Differences." *Business Horizons* 21 (August 1978):27-35. **Comparative management, Managerial functions.**

Part of a series on management and cultural differences, the emphasis here is on Indian business customs and practices.

Richman, Barry, and Copen, Melvyn. "Management Techniques in the Developing Nations." *Columbia Journal of World Business* 8 (Summer 1973):49-58. **Comparative management, Technology transfer.**

A survey of management practices in the Indian pharmaceutical industry. The measures of success are growth and profitability, but more work on social and organizational compatibility is needed.

Rose, C. J. "Management Science in the Developing Countries: A Comparative Approach to Irrigation Feasibility." *Management Science* 20 (December 1973):423-38. **Operations research and management science, Systems analysis.**

An operations research success story on an irrigation project in Burma. Water resources are popular among OR/MS/SA practitioners.

Ross, Harold et al. *Management in the Developing Countries: A Field Survey.* Report No. 72.2. Geneva: United Nations Research Institute for Social Development, 1972. **Development planning, Organization and management theory.**

A survey of management practices in developing countries. Management quality is measured against the stereotyped view of "rational" North American and West European standards.

Sagasti, Francisco R. "Management Sciences in an Underdeveloped Country: The Case of Operations Research in Peru." *Management Science* 19 (October 1972):121-31. **Operations research and management science, Control systems and techniques.**

An example of specious reasoning on the transfer of operations research techniques.

———. "Thoughts on the Use (and Abuse) of OR/MS in the Planning and Management of Development (Or: Can OR/MS Help in the Planning and Management of Revolutions?)." *Operational Research Quarterly* 27 (1976):937-48. **Operations research and management science, Development planning.**

A pragmatic look at OR/MS and the use and misuse of tools and techniques in development. This is one of the better statements on the subject.

Savage, Allan H. "Planning and Control Problems in Developing Countries." *Managerial Planning* 27 (July-August 1978):17-27. **Control systems and techniques, Planning.**

The author contends that in uncertain environments (unlike the U.S., for example) there is an even greater need for tight control systems.

Ugalde, Antonio. "A Decision Model for the Study of Public Bureaucracies." *Policy Sciences* 4 (1973):75-84. **PERT and CPM, Decision analysis.**

A modeling exercise using a case study of PERT use in the Ministry of Public Health, Colombia. Ugalde finds that PERT implementation was impeded by organizational decisionmaking.

Venu, Srinivasan. "Corporate Planning in a Developing Economy: Indian Experience." *Long Range Planning* 5 (September 1972):29-35. **Planning, Long-range planning.**

A routine report of corporate planning problems in India, with some useful insights. For example, "The corporate planner has to be a semi-astrologer." Not only in India!

Wu, Chi-Yuen. "Modern Management Techniques for Public Administration of Developing Countries." *Management Science* 15 (February 1969):B237-41. **Management in public organizations.**

An interesting editorial essay. There are some good points on the utility of "modern" management techniques in developing countries, but the statement is confused and not well-written.

RURAL DEVELOPMENT

Austin, Vincent. "Approaches to Rural Development: Lessons of a Pilot Project in Nigeria." *International Labour Review* 114 (July-August 1976):61-68. **Development planning, Project management.**

A case study with useful lessons on integration in rural development projects.

Baarspul, J. A. "The Tana Irrigation Scheme: An Integrated Development Project." *Netherlands Journal of Agricultural Science* 19 (1971):76-84. **Development planning, Project management.**

A case study with useful insights in refuting prejudices against the industriousness and managability of peasant farmers.

Chambers, Robert. *Managing Rural Development: Ideas and Experience from East Africa.* Uppsala, Sweden: Scandinavian Institute of African Studies, 1974. **Development planning, Project management.**

An outline of a rural development project management scheme in East Africa. The ideas seem sound, and the book deserves wider distribution than it has received.

Hunter, Guy. "The Implementation of Agricultural Development: Towards Criteria for the Choice of Tools." *Agricultural Administration* 1 (January 1974):51-72. **Project management, Development planning.**

An excellent article by one of the best minds in the field. There are no pat answers, but some good thinking material. **Recommended.**

Parker, Barnett R., and Srinivasan, V. "A Consumer Preference Approach to the Planning of Rural Primary Health-Care Facilities." *Operations Research* 24 (September-October 1976):991-1025. **Development planning, Analytical methods.**

A complicated model for choosing health care facility sites. Looks like methodological overkill.

Pickering, A. K. "Rural Development in Baluchistan: The Works Programme and Ground Water Supplies." *Journal of Administration Overseas* 7 (July 1968):444-53. **Development planning, Innovation.**

A case study of a self-help irrigation project in Pakistan. Pickering outlines how innovations can be diffused through such efforts.

Roumasset, James A. "Risk and Uncertainty in Agricultural Development." *Seminar Report* (of the Agricultural Development Council), no. 15 (October 1977), pp. 1-11. **Risk and uncertainty, Project management.**

A technical summary discussion of papers presented at a conference of agricultural economists.

Rutz, Henry J. "Uncertainty and the Outcome of a Development Situation." *Canadian Review of Sociology and Anthropology* 10 (1973):231-51. **Risk and uncertainty, Project management.**

A convoluted case study of rural development in Fiji. The author compares the subjective uncertainties of central planners and rural residents. There is some sensible material here, but the jargon and dense prose get in the way.

Thiesenhusen, William C. "A Cooperative Farming Project in Chile: A Case Study." *American Journal of Agricultural Economics* 48 (May 1966):295-308. **Participative management, Project management.**

A classic case study on cooperative farming projects that shows how little we have learned since the early 1960s.

Tiffen, Mary. "Timing as a Factor in the Success of Extension Programs: A Nigerian Case Study." *Agricultural Administration* 1 (April 1974):125-39. **Development planning, Project management.**

A good case study of the problem of timing in rural development.

Wade, Robert. "Leadership and Integrated Rural Development: Reflections on an Indian Success Story." *Journal of Administration Overseas* 17 (October 1978):245-55. **Economic development, Development planning.**

An account of a tentatively successful cooperative irrigation society in India. There are some very interesting lessons and social/organizational insights.

TECHNOLOGY TRANSFER

Ireson, W. Grant. "Some Problems in Technical Assistance to LDC Universities." *Technos* 4 (January-March 1975):13-23.

A preachy, simplistic "how-to-do-it" on technical assistance to LDC institutions and "living overseas."

Sangster, Raymond C. "R&D for Developing Countries." *Research Management* 22 (May 1979):34-41. **Foreign aid, Research and development.**

Sangster gives us an ill-informed presentation with no empirical content. The article is full of speculative generalizations, and he ignores much that is going on in the U.S. and in most developing countries.

Sargent, John. "The Effectiveness of Local Consultants in the Developing World." *Journal of Administration Overseas* 12 (October 1973):219-24. **Consultants.**

A short outline on how to maximize the utility of management consultants in LDCs, with sensible and sound considerations.

Sarpong, Kwame, and Rawls, James R. "A Study of the Transfer of Training from Developed to Less Developed Countries: The Case of Ghana." *Journal of Management Studies* 13 (February 1976):16-31. **Training in developing countries.**

One of the few efforts in this area, the focus is on Ghana and data are thin, but it is worth looking at.

Stoner, James A. F., and Aram, John D. "Effectiveness of Two Technical Assistance Efforts in Differing Environments." *Journal of Development Studies* 9 (July 1973):508-17. **Management in developing countries, Management effectiveness.**

Report of an experiment in placing U.S. business and law school graduates in two-year positions with private and public organizations in Latin America and Africa.

van Dam, André. "Third World Collaboration: Determining the Appropriateness of Appropriate Technology." *The Futurist* 13 (February 1979): 65-67. **Economic development.**

Once-over-lightly on the subject, with not much content but some interesting examples.

White, Lynn, Jr. "Technology Assessment from the Stance of a Medieval Historian." *Technical Forecasting and Social Change* 6 (1974):359-69. **Innovation, Systems analysis.**

A delight. This is a pragmatic historian's view of futurism, systems analysis, and technological impact assessment. History testifies to the relative imponderability of what may appear to be simple predictions.

Winpisinger, William W. "The Case Against Exporting U.S. Technology." *Research Management* 21 (March 1978):19-21. **Foreign aid, Research and development.**

A labor union president's reaction to proponents of easing LDC's access to U.S. technology. He's against it.

TRAINING IN DEVELOPING COUNTRIES

Abbas, M. B. A. "Public Administration Training in Pakistan: A Critical Appraisal." *International Review of Administrative Sciences* 36 (1970):256-70. **Management in public organizations, Administrative reform.**

A detailed examination of training strategies in Pakistan. It is difficult to appraise such efforts in the absence of empirical studies of training program results. Given the numbers of public administration training institutes in developing countries, more study is needed to inform improvements and revisions.

Adedeji, Adebayo. "Administrative Training in Africa: Problems and Development." *Philippine Journal of Public Administration* 13 (1969):11-26. **Economic development, Management in public organizations.**

An examination of administrative problems in Africa and the relative utility of training in overcoming them. The author urges the development of African institutions to train local administrators.

Akpala, Agwu. "To Rehabilitate the War Shattered Business School of the University of Nigeria." *International Review of Administrative Sciences* 37 (1971):281-85. **Management education and training, Development planning.**

A useful Nigerian perspective on needs and expectations of business school faculty and students. Akpala illustrates the persuasive influence of accepted management principles.

Casse, Pierre. "Education and Training of Executives in Developing Countries." *International Review of Administrative Sciences* 36 (1970):67-69. **Comparative management, Management education and training.**

This is a short, sensible discussion of the utility of management training programs in developing countries. The author argues for a more contextual approach, relying on problems of development rather than on perceived universals borrowed from industrialized nations.

Iboko, John I. "Management Development and Its Developing Patterns in Nigeria." *Management Review International* 16 (1976):97-104. **Management education and training, Comparative management.**

A thoughtful review of management education in Nigeria. Rather formalistic, but informative and useful, considering Nigeria's dominant position in Africa.

Ruby, Michael. "Management: The Customer Factory." *Newsweek* 86 (29 September 1975):70-71. **Consultants.**

An interesting news story on attempts by Arthur D. Little to educate future customers.

Schaffer, Bernard, ed. *Administrative Training and Development: A Comparative Study of East Africa, Zambia, Pakistan, and India.* New York: Praeger, 1974. **Comparative management, Management education and training.**

The collection is uneven, but there are so few attempts at comparing the training given LDC administrators that this book is worth a look.

Schmidt, S. C., and Scott, John T., Jr. "Advanced Training for Foreign Students: The Regional Approach." *Journal of Developing Areas* 6 (October 1971):39-50. **Management education and training, Development planning.**

A proposal for regional education centers in developing countries to reduce training costs and to focus on local and regional concerns.

Solomon, Morris J.; Heegaard, Flemming; and Kornher, Kenneth L. "An Action-Training Strategy for Project Management." *Focus: Technical Cooperation,* Special Feature 3 (1978/1), pp. 13-19. **Project management.**

A sensible strategy for training LDC project managers. Some empirical follow-up would be useful.

Tyagi, A. R. "Administrative Training: A Theoretical Postulate." *International Review of Administrative Sciences* 40 (1974):155-70. **Operations research and management science, Management in public organizations.**

A formalistic exercise, but interesting in that the principles of management science are accepted as given. The author is concerned with how best to install formal principles of administration in the Indian Civil Service and, by extension, in all developing countries.

Wu, Chi-Yuen. "Training in Public Administration for Development: Some Lessons of International Co-operation." *Journal of Administration Overseas* 10 (January 1971):12-21. **Management in public organizations.**

Examines various experiences with institutes of public administration in developing countries.

Evaluation

EVALUATION AND PROGRAM EFFECTIVENESS

Anderson, Scarvia B., and Ball, Samuel. *The Profession and Practice of Program Evaluation.* San Francisco: Jossey-Bass, 1978. **Policy analysis, Project management.**

A well-written outline of the recommended ethics and practices for a profession of program evaluation. This is one of the most sensible works on the subject.

Campbell, Donald T. "Reforms as Experiments." *American Psychologist* 24 (April 1969):409-29. **Decisionmaking, Innovation.**

Campbell's classic statement on treating social policies as experiments, with clear tests of effectiveness and an understanding that they are subject to being modified or discarded. **Recommended.**

————. "Considering the Case Against Experimental Evaluations of Social Innovations." *Administrative Science Quarterly* 15 (March 1970):110-13. **Decisionmaking.**

Campbell's response to criticisms of his proposal for experimental design of social programs. Short, but worth reading.

Dolbeare, Kenneth M., ed. *Public Policy Evaluation.* Beverly Hills, Calif.: Sage Publications, 1975. **Policy analysis.**

A collection of essays that is part of a series of yearbooks issued by the publisher. This set has a few thoughtful and useful statements on the questions raised by public policy evaluation.

Dunn, Marcus. "Government Program Evaluation Models." *Government Accountants Journal* 27 (Fall 1978):26-33. **Accounting, Management in public organizations.**

A shallow, primitive discussion of evaluation.

Fitz-Gibbon, Carol Taylor, and Morris, Lynn Lyons. *How to Design a Program Evaluation.* Beverly Hills, Calif.: Sage Publications, 1978. **Evaluation research, Analytical methods.**

This is one volume in an eight-volume *Program Evaluation Kit.* This unit is well-written and lucid and may prove useful for novices to the evaluation mystique. If the rest of the collection is as simply done, this is a worthwhile effort.

Garn, Harvey A., and Olson, Mancur. "Public Services on the Assembly Line." *Evaluation* 1 (1973):36-42. **Policy analysis.**

Two articles that look at evaluation from a public choice and collective action perspective. Well-informed cautionary statements.

Gutek, Barbara A.; Katz, Daniel; Kahn, Robert L.; and Barton, Eugenia. "Utilization and Evaluation of Government Services by the American People." *Evaluation* 2 (1974):41-48. **Management in public organizations.**

Report of a study on client perceptions in bureaucratic encounters. There are some interesting findings concerning social program design and evaluation.

Hamblin, A. C. *Evaluation and Control of Training.* London: McGraw-Hill, 1974. **Management education and training.**

This book presents a very narrow view of evaluation (as control) and training. It is interesting primarily because of the many factors that are ignored.

Hatry, Harry P. "Measuring the Effectiveness of Nondefense Public Programs." *Operations Research* 18 (September-October 1970):772-84. **Cost-benefit analysis, Organizational effectiveness.**

Some cautions on cost-benefit analysis, particularly concerning the use of a single value dimension and the elimination of "intangibles." This is but another call for clarifying objectives.

Horst, Pamela; Nay, Joe N.; Scanlon, John W.; and Wholey, Joseph S. "Program Management and the Federal Evaluator." *Public Administration Review* 34 (July-August 1974):300-308. **Management in public organizations.**

One of the better outlines of program evaluation and its meaning to program managers.

Imboden, N. *A Management Approach to Project Appraisal and Evaluation.* Paris: OECD, 1978. **Project management, Analytical methods, Developing countries.**

A formal examination of several techniques, this book has a rather extensive annotated reference list, but otherwise adds little or nothing to what is already known about appraisal and evaluation methodologies.

King, L. W.; Austin, Nancy K.; Liberman, Robert P.; and DeRisi, William J. "Accountability, Like Charity, Begins at Home." *Evaluation* 2 (1975):75-77. **Control systems and techniques, Policy analysis.**

A cursory look at a pervasive problem: How to evaluate the evaluators? The authors recognize the need, but they do not tell us how it is to be met.

Lemire, Jean-Marc. "Program Design Guidelines." *Canadian Public Administration* 20 (Winter 1977):666-78. **Analytical methods.**

A review and critique of several approaches to program design, this is primarily a listing exercise.

Mushkin, Selma J. "Evaluation: Use with Caution." *Evaluation* 1 (1973): 30-35. **Policy analysis.**

A critical look at the practice of program evaluation and its implications for policy.

Poland, Orville F. "Program Evaluation and Administrative Theory." *Public Administration Review* 34 (July-August 1974):333-38. **Decisionmaking, Policy analysis.**

An evaluation of program evaluation in public programs. Not much new.

Radin, Beryl A. "Political Relationships in Evaluation: The Case of the Experimental Schools Program." *Evaluation* 4 (1977):201-204. **Policy analysis.**

An intelligent discussion of how "politics," not "science," is the quickest path to understanding social policy.

Ridge, Warren J. "What Is Your Organization Worth?" *SAM Advanced Management Journal* 41 (Autumn 1976):15-21. **Organizational goals and objectives.**

An exercise in selling something called VAMP (value analysis of management practices). It's hard to tell whether this is a serious or tongue-in-cheek effort.

Rigby, Paul H. "Measuring Program Output." *California Management Review* 19 (Fall 1976):58-67. **Project management.**

A model for formal program selection and evaluation. Since the primary concern is with measurement, program choices are limited by assessment criteria.

Rosensteel, Robert. "Program Evaluation as an Integral Part of Public Policy." *GAO Review* 10 (Summer 1975):44-52. **Decisionmaking.**

A formalistic litany of program evaluation pap.

Rycroft, Robert W. "Selecting Policy Evaluation Criteria: Toward a Redis-covery of Public Administration." *Midwest Review of Public Administration* 12 (June 1978):87-98. **Policy analysis, Management in public organizations.**

A muddled look at program evaluation and public policy.

Schaffer, Bernard. "Policy Decisions and Institutional Evaluation." *Development and Change* 5 (1973-74):19-47. **Decision analysis, Developing countries.**

A discussion of institutions, decision systems, policy, training, and evaluation. It's never quite clear where the emphasis lies.

Soumelis, Constantin G. *Project Evaluation Methodologies and Techniques.* Paris: UNESCO, 1977. **Policy analysis.**

A primer put together for UNESCO. Adequate, but there are better efforts available.

Staats, Elmer B. "The Challenge of Evaluating Federal Social Programs." *Evaluation* 1 (1973):50-54. **Policy analysis.**

An outline of the role of the General Accounting Office (GAO) in evaluating social programs for the U.S. Congress.

Turner, Herbert D. "Principles and Methods of Program Evaluation." *Focus: Technical Cooperation* (1976/3), pp. 26-30. **Project management, Foreign aid.**

A formalistic summary of program evaluation perspectives and proce-dures in the U.S. Agency for International Development (USAID).

Wholey, Joseph S. "What Can We Actually Get from Program Evalua-tion?" *Policy Sciences* 3 (1972):361-69. **Policy analysis.**

An appraisal of the concept and the methods of program evaluation. The author, as analyst and public official, brings a unique perspective to the approach. See some of his more recent statements for changes in his views.

———; Nay, Joe N.; Scanlon, John W.; and Schmidt, Richard E. "Evalua-tion: When Is It Really Needed?" *Evaluation* 2 (1975):89-93. **Organizational objectives, Management in public organizations.**

An outline of doubtful utility on program evaluation at the program manager level.

Williams, Walter, and Elmore, Richard F., eds. *Social Program Implemen-tation.* New York: Academic Press, 1976. **Project management.**

A mixed collection. Some of the articles are better than others, but on the whole the contributors make sensible statements about implemen-tation and evaluation.

EVALUATION RESEARCH

Banner, David K. "The Politics of Evaluation Research." *Omega* 2 (1974): 763-74. **Evaluation and program effectiveness, Analytical methods.**

The author acknowledges that evaluation research is essentially political and urges that it be depoliticized; but there is no help on how this is to be done.

Bernstein, Ilene Nagel, and Freeman, Howard E. *Academic and Entrepreneurial Research: The Consequences of Diversity in Federal Evaluation Studies*. New York: Russell Sage Foundation, 1975. **Evaluation and program effectiveness, Policy analysis.**

Based on studies done for the NIH and NIMH, this is an excellent examination of the relative technical merit of employing a university-based evaluation team or a private consulting firm.

Caro, Francis G., ed. *Readings in Evaluation Research*. New York: Russell Sage Foundation, 1971. **Evaluation and program effectiveness, Policy analysis.**

One of the best books of readings on evaluation, and probably the most popular. It provides an excellent if dated overview of program evaluation strategies and theory.

Freeman, Howard E. "The Present Status of Evaluation Research." United Nations Educational, Scientific and Cultural Organization, Report SS.76/WS/10 (August 1976), pp. 1-71. **Policy analysis.**

A detailed state-of-the-art paper on evaluation by one of the leading figures in the discipline. Interesting overview.

O'Toole, Richard, ed. *The Organization, Management and Tactics of Social Research*. Cambridge, Mass.: Schenkman Publishing, 1971. **Organizational goals and objectives.**

A good collection, covering many aspects of evaluation research. Edward Suchman's article (chapter 5) is particularly useful.

Weiss, Carol H. *Evaluation Research: Methods of Assessing Program Effectiveness*. Englewood Cliffs, N.J.: Prentice-Hall, 1972. **Evaluation and program effectiveness, Analytical methods.**

An intelligent, thorough primer, this is one of the best books on the subject for the uninitiated. Weiss is a leading scholar/practitioner in the field, and knows whereof she speaks. If you want only one book on evaluation, it should be this one. **Recommended.**

―――. "Between the Cup and the Lip. . . ." *Evaluation* 1 (1973):49-55. **Project management, Policy analysis.**

Results of a study Weiss did for the U.S. National Institute for Mental Health (NIMH). She concludes that evaluation serves a real political function that is not always intended.

————. "Where Politics and Evaluation Research Meet." *Evaluation* 1 (1973):37-45. **Project management, Policy analysis.**

An intelligent summary of the politics of evaluation by one of the stars of the profession. This article provides a good balance to much of the methodological jargon that is usually published.

Weiss, Robert S., and Rein, Martin. "The Evaluation of Broad-Aim Programs: A Cautionary Case and a Moral." *Annals* 385 (September 1969): 133-42. **Evaluation and program effectiveness, Organizational learning.**

An early critique of the methodological focus in evaluation research. Much has been written since 1969, but little progress is evident.

————. "The Evaluation of Broad-Aim Programs: Experimental Design, Its Difficulties, and an Alternative." *Administrative Science Quarterly* 15 (March 1970):97-109. **Evaluation and program effectiveness.**

An excellent primer on the uses and limitations of evaluation research. **Recommended.**

PERFORMANCE APPRAISAL

Patton, Arch. "Does Performance Appraisal Work?" *Business Horizons* 16 (February 1973):83-91. **Management effectiveness, Evaluation and program effectiveness.**

A formal statement about the need for executives to maximize profit as a prime indicator of effectiveness—a startling disclosure.

Rogers, Robert T. "Performance Appraisals: Why Don't They Work Better?" *GAO Review* (Fall 1975), pp. 73-81. **Management effectiveness, Control systems and techniques.**

A vapid evaluation of performance appraisal.

Management

COMPARATIVE MANAGEMENT

Azrael, Jeremy R. *Managerial Power and Soviet Politics*. Cambridge, Mass.: Harvard University Press, 1966. **Control systems and techniques.**

An excellent study of the role management expertise plays in Soviet industry. The classic "Red" vs. "expert" dichotomy is discussed and examined.

Ballon, Robert J. "Understanding the Japanese." *Business Horizons* 13 (June 1970):21-30. **Organizational design, Organization and management theory.**

A good outline of Japanese management style and government, organization, and social relationships.

————. "A Lesson from Japan: Contract, Control, and Authority." *Journal of Contemporary Business* 8 (1979):27-35. **Organizational control, Organizational behavior.**

Another comparative look at Japanese views on business practices.

Boddewyn, J., and Nath, R. "Comparative Management Studies: An Assessment." *Management International Review* 10 (1970):3-11.

A literature review with a good bibliography of pre-1969 materials.

Crozier, Michel. "Attitudes of French Managers Regarding the Administration of Their Firms." *International Studies of Management and Organization* 3 (Fall 1978):39-63. **Organization and management theory, Management policy, strategy, and style.**

An excellent though necessarily limited study of attitudes that may not be wholly "French." More *comparative* work is needed.

Dickerman, Allen. *Training Japanese Managers.* New York: Praeger, 1974. **Management education and training.**

A rather formal treatment of a subject that has been of great interest in recent years. The interest has waned as we have learned that there is no magic in Japan either.

Drucker, Peter F. "What We Can Learn from Japanese Management." *Harvard Business Review* 49 (March-April 1971):110-22. **Organization and management theory.**

A good examination of alternative organizational forms by one of the biggest names in the management business.

Fuchs, Victor R., ed. *Policy Issues and Research Opportunities in Industrial Organization.* New York: National Bureau of Economic Research, 1972. **Organization and management theory, Organizational design.**

A mixed collection of essays. The Richard R. Nelson piece is a particularly insightful statement on the mistaken view of the firm as a rational, predictable actor in a well-defined environment.

"Japanese Managers Tell How Their System Works." *Fortune* 96 (November 1977):126-38. **Managerial functions.**

Conversations with Japanese managers. This is an interesting, lightweight piece that may improve understanding—but not by much.

Johnson, Richard Tanner, and Ouchi, William G. "Made in America (under Japanese Management)." *Harvard Business Review* 52 (September-October 1974):61-69. **Personnel management.**

Another review of Japanese management practices. Nothing succeeds like success.

Kobayashi, Maurie K., and Burke, Warner W. "Organization Development in Japan." *Columbia Journal of World Business* 11 (Summer 1976):113-23. **Organizational development.**

Another Japanese adaptation (improvement?) of a Western management technique.

Maunders, K. T. "Financial Management in the Soviet Industrial Enterprise." *Accounting and Business Research,* no. 8 (Autumn 1972), pp. 298-307. **Accounting, Decisionmaking.**

An examination of accounting and business practices in the Soviet Union. The author concludes that advances or improvements will depend on political events rather than on increased knowledge.

McNulty, Nancy G. "European Management Education Comes of Age." *Conference Board Record* 12 (December 1975):38-43. **Management education and training.**

A review of the independent directions taken by many European institutions.

Michel, A. J., and Permut, S. E. "Management Science in the United States and Europe: A Decade of Change in the Literature." *Omega* 6 (1978):43-51. **Operations research and management science, Control systems and techniques.**

A literature review to illustrate a shift away from implementation articles in three prestigious journals.

Nath, Raghu. "Comparative Management and Organization Theory: Linking the Two." *Organization and Administrative Sciences* 5 (1974-75):115-24. **Organization and management theory.**

A formal academic discussion, of little use to researchers or managers.

Negandhi, Anant R. "Comparative Management and Organization Theory: A Marriage Needed." *Academy of Management Journal* 18 (1975):334-44. **Organization and management theory.**

A review of the literature and an attempt to develop an "integrating model." The author gives us nothing new or particularly insightful.

Newman, William H. "Is Management Exportable?" *Columbia Journal of World Business* 5 (January-February 1970):7-18. **Organization and management theory, Management education and training.**

An examination of some of the cultural premises underlying U.S. management practices. The author also attempts to determine their applicability to other environments.

Oh, Taik. "Japanese Management: A Critical Review." *Academy of Management Review* 1 (January 1976):14-25. **Organizational structure, Management models.**

An excellent examination of how Japanese firms' employer/employee relationships reduce uncertainty for both.

Peterson, Richard B., and Shimada, Justin Y. "Sources of Management Problems in Japanese-American Joint Ventures." *Academy of Management Review* 3 (October 1978):796-804. **Management policy, strategy, and style, Organization and management theory.**

Another discussion of differences between U.S. and Japanese organizations and management styles.

Reimann, Bernard C. "Management Concern, Context, and Structure: An Open-Systems Model for Comparative Organization Research." *Quarterly Journal of Management Development* 4 (March 1973):43-61. **Organizational effectiveness, Organizational structure, Organization and management theory.**

The author presents a multi-variate model, combining contextual, structural, and task environment to improve predictors of organizational effectiveness.

Rohan, Thomas M. "Europeans in America Practice 'Foreign' Management." *Industry Week* 200 (January 1979):64-67. **Management policy, strategy, and style, Organizational design.**

A cursory scan of European management practices. This might be a useful area for further research now that some large U.S. corporations are foreign-controlled.

Simonetti, Jack L., and Simonetti, Frank L. "American and Italian Management Policy Toward Task Environment Agents: Is There a Difference?" *Management International Review* 17 (January 1977):77-85. **Management theory.**

A confusing article that is more concerned with methodology than the research question. The results are therefore puzzling.

Tannenbaum, Arnold S. et al. *Hierarchy in Organizations: An International Comparison.* San Francisco: Jossey-Bass, 1974. **Organization and management theory, Organizational control.**

A consideration of the various functions of organizational hierarchy. This is one of the few examinations of what is for many *the* organizing principle.

Trepo, Georges. "Management Style à la Française." *European Business,* no. 39 (Autumn 1973), pp. 71-79. **Management by objective.**

A perceptive exercise in comparative national management style.

van Nieuwenhuijze, C. A. O. "Public Administration, Comparative Administration, Development Administration: Concepts and Theory in Their Struggle for Relevance." *Development and Change* 5 (1973-74):1-18. **Management in developing countries, Management in public organizations.**

A literature review; elliptical, and full of jargon.

Vogel, Ezra F., ed. *Modern Japanese Organization and Decision-Making.* Berkeley: University of California Press, 1975. **Managerial functions, Decisionmaking.**

A modest collection that is intended to inform. It does the job.

Zand, Dale. "Management in Israel." *Business Horizons* 21 (August 1978): 36-47. **Managerial functions, Developing countries.**

A useful survey of Israeli managers' methods of handling turbulent change to assure some degree of stability.

CONTINGENCY THEORY

Cherns, Albert B. "Can Behavioral Science Help Design Organizations?" *Organizational Dynamics* 5 (Spring 1977):44-64. **Organizational design.**

Another modification of "contingency" theory, with still another list of principles. The author argues that his list is not prescriptive, but serves only as a "guide."

Collins, Frank, and Willingham, John J. "Contingency Management Approach to Budgeting." *Management Accounting* 59 (September 1977):45-48. **Participative management, Budgeting.**

A psychological model of participatory budgeting, with little content.

Duncan, Robert B. "The Implementation of Different Decision Making Structures in Adapting to Environmental Uncertainty: An Expansion of Contingency Theories of Organization." *Academy of Management Proceeding* 31 (1971):39-47. **Organization and management theory, Risk and uncertainty.**

Some confusing use of concepts, but the author's idea of a self-organizing system is interesting.

Hofer, Charles W. "Toward a Contingency Theory of Business Strategy." *Academy of Management Journal* 18 (December 1975):784-810. **Management policy, strategy, and style, Operations research and management science.**

An academic treatise that is very hard going. It may not be worth the effort.

Kast, Fremont E. and Rosenzweig, James E. *Contingency Views of Organization and Management*. Chicago: Science Research Associates, 1973. **Organization and management theory, Management policy, strategy, and style.**

Probably the best single collection of materials on contingency theory. The authors have knitted together a diverse set of essays into a coherent statement on organizational tasks and environment. **Recommended.**

Longenecker, Justin G., and Pringle, Charles D. "The Illusion of Contingency Theory as a General Theory"; and Luthans, Fred, and Stewart, Todd I. "The Reality or Illusion of a General Contingency Theory of Management: A Response to the Longenecker and Pringle Critique." *Academy of Management Review* 3 (July 1978):679-87. **Organization and management theory, Organizational structure.**

A critique of general contingency theory (GCT) and a response—both in the same issue. Both are short and worth looking at if GCT is an interest.

McMahon, J. Timothy, and Perritt, G. W. "Toward a Contingency Theory of Organizational Control." *Academy of Management Journal* 16 (December 1973):624-35. **Organizational control, Organizational effectiveness.**

Another statement on the subject—this time linked to degrees of "total control" in organizations.

Morse, John J., and Lorsch, Jay W. "Beyond Theory Y." *Harvard Business Review* 48 (May-June 1970):61-68. **Organizational design, Personnel management.**

One of the earlier statements on contingency theory, this is a nice introduction if you are unfamiliar with more recent developments.

Shepard, Jon M., and Hougland, James G., Jr. "Contingency Theory: 'Complex Man' or 'Complex Organization'?" *Academy of Management Review* 3 (July 1978):413-27. **Organizational design, Organization and management theory.**

A good examination of contingency theories of organization. The authors advocate more integration of various theoretical approaches, but it is not clear why. Excellent bibliography.

Shetty, Y. K. "Contingency Management: Current Perspectives for Managing Organizations." *Management International Review* 14 (1974):27-35. **Management effectiveness, Organization and management theory.**

A summary statement on "contingency" views of management. This is useful as an introduction and to supplement other readings in this area.

————, and Carlisle, Howard M. "A Contingency Model of Organizational Design." *California Management Review* 15 (Fall 1972):38-45. **Organizational design, Organization and management theory.**

More on contingency. This is useful if you are interested in this particular approach.

MANAGEMENT BY OBJECTIVES

Albrecht, Karl. "The Myths and Realities of MBO." *Management Awareness Program* 4 (September-October 1978):63-82. **Organizational effectiveness, Control systems and techniques.**

In one of the more intelligent examinations of MBO, the author provides a sensible outline of the most common MBO pitfalls. His advice is to "Think Big, but Start Small."

Aplin, John C., Jr.; Schoderbek, Charles G.; and Schoderbek, Peter P. "Tough-Minded Management by Objectives." *Human Resource Management* 18 (Summer 1979):9-13. **Organization and management theory, Management models.**

The authors examine five "fallacies" of MBO implementation and suggest that clear expectations, fairness, and rewards will provide success. The description of the mistaken assumptions is sensible and apparently well-founded; the prescription for MBO achievement is simplistic and misleading.

Babcock, Richard, and Sørenson, Peter F., Jr. "An MBO Checklist: Are Conditions Right for Implementation?" *Management Review* 68 (June 1979):59-62. **Project management, Control systems and techniques.**

A useless exercise. If an organization met all the requirements of the checklist, it would not need MBO or any other gimmick.

Beam, Henry H. "Bringing MBO Back to Basics." *Supervisory Management* 24 (July 1979):25-30. **Control systems and techniques.**

Another ritualistic account of how to "save" MBO.

Dirsmith, Mark W., and Jablonsky, Stephen F. "MBO in the Public Sector: A Conceptual Examination." *American Institute for Decision Sciences: Proceedings* (1977), p. 595. **Control systems and techniques, Management in public organizations.**

A short but very perceptive analysis of MBO in public organizations. The authors argue that the technique is most useful in stable, known environments where objectives are non-contentious.

Fri, Robert W. "How to Manage the Government for Results: The Rise of MBO." *Organizational Dynamics* 2 (Spring 1974):19-33. **Management in public organizations, Organizational goals and objectives.**

The author provides some sensible rules of thumb that conflict with the prescriptions he offers. Worth reading.

Futrell, Charles M. et al. "Benefits and Problems in a Salesforce MBO System." *Industrial Marketing Management* 6 (1977):265-72. **Management policy, strategy, and style, Control systems and techniques.**

An inconclusive study of the short-term effects of MBO on a salesforce in a relatively limited market.

Hopkins, David M. "Improving MBO Through Synergistics." *Public Personnel Management* 8 (May-June 1979):163-68. **Management effectiveness, Personnel management.**

Lots of fluff and verbiage around another "how to improve MBO" statement. This time it's to be done with nominal group technique (NGT) or Delphi.

Humble, John. "Avoiding the Pitfalls of the MBO Trap." *European Business,* no. 27 (Autumn 1970), pp. 13-20. **Control systems and techniques, Planning.**

A trivial piece illustrating how the prerequisites for a system (or innovation) are a major obstacle to its adoption. When you reach a point where MBO can be used, you don't need it.

Jacobs, Charles E., Jr. "MBO and Public Management." *Government Accountants Journal* 27 (Winter 1978):5-11. **Control systems and techniques, Management in public organizations.**

A chronicle of MBO in the Federal government, with a mild critique of the control ideal implicit in the technique's application in public organizations.

Jamieson, Bruce D. "Behavioral Problems with Management by Objectives." *Academy of Management Journal* 16 (September 1973):496-505. **Managerial functions, Organization and management theory.**

An inconclusive critique of MBO from a human relations perspective.

Mayer, Richard J. "The Secret Life of MBO." *Human Resource Management* 17 (Fall 1978):6-11. **Analytical methods, Organization and management theory.**

MBO, self-discovery, and "relationships." The secret is safe.

McConkie, Mark L. "A Clarification of the Goal Setting and Appraisal Processes in MBO." *Academy of Management Review* 4 (January 1979):29-40. **Organizational goals and objectives, Performance appraisal, Control systems and techniques.**

A more current statement of the confusion about MBO. This article has an excellent bibliography, but no new information.

Molander, C. F. "Management by Objectives in Perspective." *Journal of Management Studies* 9 (February 1972):74-81. **Management control, Organizational development.**

An examination of a case study to illustrate how MBO is easily converted to a hierarchic control system. Short, but interesting.

Nelson, Charles A. "Does Management by Objectives Make Sense for Colleges and Universities?" *Management Focus* 26 (March-April 1979):9-13. **Management policy, strategy, and style, Control systems and techniques.**

An intelligent critique of MBO. Though the focus is on universities, the questions raised apply to MBO applications in any organization.

Nystrom, Paul C. "Save MBO by Disowning It!" *Personnel Journal* 56 (August 1977):391-93. **Personnel management.**

Another short statement on how to save MBO programs. I do not see how charts or lists will help.

Odiorne, George S. "The Politics of Implementing MBO." *Business Horizons* 17 (June 1974):13-21. **Control systems and techniques, Management effectiveness.**

This can be compared with some of the author's later work. He was and remains a staunch defender of MBO—against all "haters."

―――. "MBO in the 1980s: Will It Survive?" *Management Review* 66 (July 1977):30-42. **Control systems and techniques, Management effectiveness.**

Another article extolling the virtues of MBO and condemning the mossbacks who continue to resist it.

―――. "MBO: A Backward Glance." *Business Horizons* 21 (October 1978):14-24. **Management history, Organization and management theory.**

A survey of the academic and organizational history of MBO. Interestingly, Odiorne thinks if you're not for MBO you're against it; he classifies skeptics (or others who question MBO) as "haters." Nothing is said about evidence.

Reed, Preston Turner. "Management by Objectives: Bridge Between Present and Future." *Directors and Boards* 1 (Spring 1976):44-48. **Organizational goals and objectives, Control systems and techniques.**

Though too short to be very useful, this article has a good bibliography.

Ryan, Edward J., Jr. "Federal Government MBO: Another Managerial Fad?" *MSU Business Topics* 24 (Autumn 1976):35-43. **Management in public organizations, Control systems and techniques.**

An examination of the actual uses made of techniques like MBO. The author asks if federal MBO is another case of installing a poorly understood procedure in order to appear up-to-date.

Schnake, Melvin. "Management by Objectives: Review and Evaluation." *Managerial Planning* 27 (March-April 1979):19 **Control systems and techniques, Management policy, strategy, and style.**

A short, formal literature survey. This is an adequate, quick review of the arguments for and against management by objectives.

Shetty, Y. Krishna, and Carlisle, Howard M. "Organizational Correlates of a Management by Objectives Program." *Academy of Management Journal* 17 (March 1974):155-60.

A shallow study that presents scant evidence for or against MBO as a management tool.

Sokolik, Stanley L. "Feedback and Control: The Hollow in MBO Practice." *Human Resource Management* 17 (Winter 1978):23-28. **Information processing, Control systems and techniques.**

An MBO "expert" (and consultant) tells why it doesn't work—but not how it can.

Steers, Richard M., and Spencer, Daniel G. "Achievement Needs and MBO Goal-Setting." *Personnel Journal* 57 (January 1978):26-28. **Personnel management, Control systems and techniques.**

Another look at MBO and why it has not worked very well. This time we are told that workers have varying levels of need for achievement.

Weihrich, Heinz. "MBO in Four Management Systems." *MSU Business Topics* 24 (Autumn 1976):51-56. **Organizational design, Management policy, strategy, and style, Superior-subordinate relationship.**

Another exploration of why MBO doesn't work, with a plea for understanding the organization before installing MBO.

————. "Getting Action into MBO." *Journal of Systems Management* 28 (November 1977):10-13. **Planning, Organizational design.**

Still selling MBO. Now we need something called "action plans"?

West, George Edward. "Bureaupathology and the Failure of MBO." *Human Resource Management* 16 (Summer 1977):33-40. **Organizational psychology, Control systems and techniques.**

The psychology of MBO: It fails because there is something wrong with the people. The author never questions the technique; maybe it's the wrong medicine.

MANAGEMENT CONSULTANTS

Archer, John F. "Getting the Most Out of Management Consultants." *European Business*, no. 42 (Autumn 1974), pp. 34-41. **Problem solving, Evaluation and program effectiveness.**

Some information and a few good ideas, along with some ill-considered recommendations.

Downs, Anthony. "Some Thoughts on Giving People Economic Advice." *American Behavioral Scientist* 9 (September 1965):30-32. **Decision-making, Organizational learning.**

An intelligent discussion of the uses to which "expert" economic advice can be put. Not so surprisingly, most of them have little to do with economics.

Mosley, Donald C. "Professional Ethics and Competence in Management Consulting." *California Management Review* 12 (Spring 1970):44-48. **Management effectiveness, Organizational learning.**

A cautionary tale on the potential problems in hiring consultants and following their recommendations.

Wortman, Max S., Jr., and Forst, Leland J. "Monitoring Consultant Activities: A Revealing Analysis." *Academy of Management Proceedings* (1973), pp. 172-78. **Management policy, strategy, and style.**

The author explains how to use an independent monitor to check on outside consultants. A short but useful guide on how to detect charlatans.

MANAGEMENT EDUCATION AND TRAINING

Anderson, Lane K. "Systems Education to Match Employers' Needs." *Journal of Systems Management* 28 (November 1977):6-9. **Systems analysis.**

Short, with little content. This is typical of articles that make broad generalizations on employers' needs based on a small biased sample.

Anthony, Robert N.; Dearden, John; and Vancil, Richard F. *Management Control Systems: Text, Cases and Readings.* Rev. ed. Homewood, Ill.: Richard D. Irwin, 1972. **Management control, Organization and management theory.**

A popular text that illustrates the mainstream approach to management education. This is one of the best of the management control texts.

Carrithers, Wallace M., and Weinwurm, E. H. *Business Information and Accounting Systems.* Columbus, Ohio: C. E. Merrill, 1967. **Control systems, Analytical methods.**

A somewhat dated text that provides an excellent view of what was being taught in business courses through the sixties. Things have changed, but not much.

Cook, James R. "Management Training? Don't Waste Your Money!" *Supervisory Management* 23 (February 1978):30-37. **Consultants.**

A lightweight piece that is not particularly useful since the major recommendation is to "do the right thing."

Culbert, Samuel A. "The Real World and the Management Classroom." *California Management Review* 19 (Summer 1977):65-78. **Organization and management theory.**

An excellent piece. The author is both a teacher and a practicing consultant. He points out disparities between students' and managers' expectations and the possible. **Recommended.**

Denning, Basil. "Lost in the Management Education Jungle." *European Business,* no. 42 (Autumn 1974), pp. 42-46. **Consultants.**

A short, lightweight, but somewhat useful guide to problems of management training.

Duncan, W. Jack. "Methodological Orientations and Management Theory: An Analysis of Academic Opinion." *Academy of Management Journal* 13 (September 1970):337-48. **Organization and management theory.**

A study of the effect of geography (location) on management education. Where the school *is* in large part determines the influence of empiricism in management (business) education.

Dyer, William G. "What Makes Sense in Management Training?" *Management Review* 67 (June 1978):50-56. **Managerial functions, Organizational objectives.**

A sensible review of our search for management universals that can be taught in training programs. The author reaches no conclusions, but makes some interesting comments.

Foy, Nancy. "Action Learning Comes to Industry." *Harvard Business Review* 55 (September-October 1977):158-68. **Organizational learning.**

An astute observer's report on a British firm's experience with a "learn by doing" problem-solving program. Some interesting information.

Gordon, Paul J. "The Unfinished Business of Business Education." *Record* 13 (January 1976):60-64. **Management effectiveness.**

A commentary on U.S. and European business schools by an American professor of business. There is some cogent criticism of the ability of such schools to prepare students for executive positions.

Gruber, W. H., and Niles, J. S. "Research and Experience in Management." *Business Horizons* 16 (August 1973):15-24. **Problem solving.**

In this sensible article, Gruber and Niles discuss how tasks can shift from programmed to non-programmed and the need for managers to keep pace with changes.

Guyot, James F. "Management Training and Post-Industrial Apologetics." *California Management Review* 20 (Summer 1978):84-93. **Evaluation and program effectiveness, Managerial functions.**

Another wordy but intelligent assessment of efforts to evaluate management training and development programs.

Hague, Hawdon. "Just How Useful Are Courses?" *Industrial Management* (UK) (January 1977), pp. 17-18. **Managerial functions.**

A short, scathing critique of the management course jungle. This is an excellent comment on the real problems in management training courses.

Hand, Herbert H. "The Mystery of Executive Education." *Business Horizons* 14 (June 1971):35-38. **Management effectiveness.**

Another piece on how to develop "good" managers. It is difficult to understand how this can be done without really knowing what it is that managers do.

Hodge, B. J.; Anthony, William P.; and Swindle, Orson. "Management Development: 12 Months Later." *Personnel Administrator* 21 (September 1976):49-55. **Evaluation and program effectiveness.**

Report on an evaluation of a management development program. There is some useful information, but it is not particularly insightful.

Hodgetts, Richard M., and Barton-Dobenin, J. "Management Training Programs: Who Uses Them and Why?" *Academy of Management Proceedings* (1973), pp. 189-92.

If you want some ideas on how to sensibly evaluate a management training program, don't expect to find them in this article.

Livingston, J. Sterling. "Myth of the Well-Educated Manager." *Harvard Business Review* 52 (January-February 1974):79-89. **Management effectiveness.**

A discussion of business school curricula, student performance, and success records in actual management. The conclusions are echoed and supported by other work. **Recommended.**

Lynn, Laurence E., Jr. "Organizing Human Services in Florida Teaching Public Policy." *Evaluation* 3 (1976):91-97. **Management in public organizations.**

This is interesting because of the student responses to their task of "managing" social service reorganization in Florida. They saw a need to "beat" the bureaucracy.

Maxon, Richard C., and Stone, Kenneth E. "A Strategy for Developing Effective Management Training." *Journal of Small Business Management* 15 (July 1977):9-14. **Managerial functions, Organization and management theory.**

A confusing outline of a potential approach to management training. The authors concentrate on the formal "principles," which lead them into deceptive prescriptions.

Salaman, Graeme. "Management Development and Organization Theory." *Journal of European Industrial Training* 2 (1978):7-11. **Organization and management theory, Organizational control.**

A good analysis of the management/control distinction. The author rejects the classical "rational" organization theories as prescriptive and of little use in understanding the dynamics of real organizations. **Recommended.**

Sawbridge, D., and Keithley, G. R. "Industrial Relations Training for Shop Stewards: Training without Objectives." *Management Decisions* 14 (1976):148-60. **Comparative management, Organizational psychology.**

A short look at the role of shop stewards in British corporations.

Sayles, Leonard. "Whatever Happened to Management? Or, Why the Dull Stepchild." *Business Horizons* 3 (April 1970):25-34. **Managerial functions, Decisionmaking.**

One of the most intelligent and intelligible authorities in the field discusses management education and the disparities between it and practice. **Recommended.**

Schmidt, Warren H. "How to Evaluate a Company's Training Efforts." *California Management Review* 12 (Spring 1970):49-56. **Evaluation and program effectiveness, Managerial functions.**

Interesting in that the "evaluation" reveals nothing. The author claims that training is "important," yet he provides no basis for this assertion.

Selby, Brian. "The Modern Military Model." *Management Today* (April 1978), p. 70. **Management models.**

An examination of the recruiting and management development policies of the British armed forces and industry. Apparently there is much to be learned.

Shetty, Y. K., and Peery, Newman S. "Are Top Executives Transferable Across Companies?" *Business Horizons* 19 (June 1976):23-28. **Management effectiveness.**

An informative article. The data are thin, but the findings are interesting. Chief executive officers promoted from within the firm are more effective than those recruited from outside.

Wooldredge, William D. "Fast Tracking Programs for MBAs: Do They Really Work?" *Management Review* 68 (April 1979):9-13. **Managerial functions.**

A narrow statement on how one corporation (B. F. Goodrich) uses MBAs. This has little of general interest.

Wortman, Max S. "Shifts in the Conceptual Approaches Which Underlie Principles of Management." *Academy of Management Journal* 13 (December 1970):437-48. **Management models, Organization and management theory.**

An outline of shifts in the content of management courses and texts. Good bibliography.

Wren, Daniel A.; Atherton, Roger M.; and Michaelsen, Larry K. "The Managerial Experience of Management Professors: Are the Blind Leading the Blind?" *Journal of Management* 4 (1978):75-83. **Management effectiveness, Managerial functions.**

A report of a faculty survey of 21 "best" business schools. Professors in these schools do have managerial experience, but it's in not-for-profit organizations or is pre-1970. It is not clear what this means for potential MBAs.

Zeira, Yoram. "The Systems Approach to Management Development: Studies in Frustration and Failure." *Organizational Dynamics* 3 (Fall 1974):65-80. **Systems approach, Organizational growth and change.**

A case study of a failure of management to understand organizational constraints. The management development program that was installed did not change as the organization grew and changed.

MANAGEMENT EFFECTIVENESS

Dowling, William, ed. *Effective Management and the Behavioral Sciences.* New York: AMACOM, 1978. **Organization and management theory, Management policy, strategy, and style.**

Conversations with various "big names" in management and the behavioral sciences: Drucker, Skinner, Homans, Likert, Argyris, McClelland, Beer, Boulding, and Bennis. Reprinted from *Organization Dynamics, Management Review,* and similar journals.

Greenberg, George D. "The Coordinating Roles of Management: A Typology for Analysis." *Midwest Review of Public Administration* 10 (June 1976):67-76. **Organizational objectives, Organizational conflict.**

A short examination of the various managerial tactics used to avoid or to resolve conflict. This is not a detailed analysis, but a helpful classification effort.

Greiner, Larry E.; Leitch, Paul D.; and Barnes, Louis B. "Putting Judgment Back into Decisions." *Harvard Business Review* 48 (March-April 1970):59-67. **Decision analysis, Information systems.**

Some very interesting findings on centralization, decisionmaking, and field unit evaluation (p. 64).

Heller, Robert. "The Future of Management." *Management Today* (UK) (December 1976), pp. 54-57. **Organizational growth and change, Management policy, strategy, and style.**

A speculative exercise that forecasts a return to common sense in managing. I hope he's right.

MANAGEMENT HISTORY

Chandler, Alfred D., Jr. *Strategy and Structure: Chapters in the History of the Industrial Enterprise.* Cambridge, Mass.: The MIT Press, 1962. **Organizational structure, Organization and management theory.**

A classic work on American industrial history. Chandler's book provides a better understanding of how a few major industrial firms (General Motors, Du Pont, Standard Oil [N.J.], and Sears) grew and prospered. **Recommended.**

————. *The Visible Hand.* Cambridge, Mass.: Belknap Press, 1977. **Managerial functions, Organization and management theory.**

An account of the growth of large-scale businesses in the U.S. from the 1850s to the 1920s. Chandler attributes this development to the visible hand of management replacing the invisible hand of market forces. A fascinating book. **Recommended.**

Crowther, J. G., and Whiddington, R. *Science at War.* New York: Philosophical Library, 1948. **Operations research and management science, Analytical methods.**

A fascinating account of how operations research started in Britain in the early days of World War II. Long out of print, this book is worth looking for. Also see R. V. Jones, *The Wizard War.* **Recommended.**

George, Claude S., Jr. *The History of Management Thought.* Englewood Cliffs, N.J.: Prentice-Hall, 1968. **Organization and management theory, Managerial functions.**

Probably the most popular history of management; but it should be read along with Wren, Chandler, and Mouzelis.

Giglioni, Giovanni B., and Bedeian, Arthur G. "A Conspectus of Management Control Theory: 1900-1972." *Academy of Management Journal* 17 (June 1974):292-305. **Organization and management theory, Management control.**

A literature survey, with an excellent bibliography, that tentatively explores the control emphasis in organization and management theory.

Hitch, Charles. "An Appreciation of Systems Analysis." *Operations Research* 3 (November 1955):466-81. **Systems analysis, Operations research and management science.**

A classic, this piece must be read by all seriously interested in OR/MS/SA. A companion to Blackett's work, Crowther and Whiddington's *Science at War,* and Jones's *The Wizard War.*

Jacob, Herbert. *German Administration Since Bismarck*. New Haven, Conn.: Yale University Press, 1963. **Bureaucracy.**

One of the best histories of the development of modern bureaucratic organization in Germany. Jacob provides useful background to understanding bureaucratic growth elsewhere.

Jones, R. V. *The Wizard War*. New York: Coward, McCann, & Geoghegan, 1978. **Managerial functions, Management effectiveness.**

This is a marvelous book. It's a factual account of British scientific intelligence activities during World War II. There are some very interesting observations on how uncertain tasks are made manageable. Jones also offers some comments on P. M. S. Blackett's operations research unit. **Highly recommended.**

Koontz, Harold. "The Management Theory Jungle." *Academy of Management Journal* 4 (December 1961):174-88. **Managerial functions, Organization and management theory.**

One of the later classics, this is an excellent introduction and an early critique that is still valid. **Recommended.**

Parsons, H. McIlvaine. "What Caused the Hawthorne Effect?" *Administration and Society* 10 (1978):259-83. **Organization and management theory, Organizational behavior.**

A marvelously revealing article. The "Hawthorne effect" that has been the subject of so much human relations activity was in fact the result of information feedback and piecework rates. The author argues that operant conditioning techniques were the implicit reasons for production increases. **Recommended.**

Steinhardt, Jacinto. "The Role of OR in the Navy." *U.S. Naval Institute: Proceedings* 72 (May 1946):649-55. **Operations research and management science.**

A classic statement on the pragmatic uses of OR in the early days. This article is worth a look, if only to maintain perspective.

Urwick, L. F. "Papers in the Science of Administration." *Academy of Management Journal* 13 (December 1970):361-71. **Management in public organizations, Organization and management theory.**

A witty, well-written defense by one of the co-editors of the classic "Papers." Urwick generally argues that no one has come up with anything better since 1937. He may have a point, but that just shows how little we have learned about management.

———. "Semantic Hay—The Word 'Organization'." *Omega* 1 (1973):97-105. **Organization and management theory, Organizational design.**

Nothing new. Urwick just wanted to let us know he's still around.

Wrege, Charles D., and Perroni, Amedeo G. "Taylor's Pig-Tale: A Historical Analysis of Frederick W. Taylor's Pig-Iron Experiments." *Academy of Management Journal* 17 (March 1974):6-27. **Organization and management theory, Operations research and management science.**

A fascinating historical study that should serve to refute the empirical basis of F. W. Taylor's work. So far this piece has had little impact.

————, and Stotka, Anne Marie. "Cooke Creates a Classic: The Story Behind F. W. Taylor's Principles of Scientific Management." *Academy of Management Review* 3 (October 1978):736-49. **Operations research and management science, Organization and management theory.**

A well-researched exposé arguing that F. W. Taylor did not write *Principles of Scientific Management*.

Wren, Daniel A. *The Evolution of Management Thought.* New York: Ronald Press, 1972. **Organization and management theory, Managerial functions.**

A marvelous book. A scholarly approach combined with lucid writing is a guarantee of quality. One of the best books on management theory and its effect on practice. **Recommended.**

MANAGEMENT IN PUBLIC ORGANIZATIONS

Bergeron, Pierre G. "Why Government Managers Aren't More Productive: Too Many Controls and Not Enough Say Dulls Their Effectiveness." *CA Magazine* 111 (June 1978):39-43. **Management effectiveness, Control systems and techniques.**

An interesting review of the impact of a control emphasis in Canadian government.

Boschken, Herman L. "Organizational Logic for Concurrent Government in Metropolitan Areas." *Academy of Management Review* 1 (January 1976):5-13. **Organization and management theory.**

A bit confusing, but this is an interesting argument for "intermediate" organizational forms to handle complex urban problems. (Also see Landau, "Linkage, Coding, and Intermediacy.")

Chartrand, Robert Lee. "Congressional Management and Use of Information Technology." *Journal of Systems Management* 29 (August 1978):10-15. **Information systems, Computer services.**

The Congress is presented as "user" in this description of the various computer assisted systems operated by the Congressional Research Service (CRS). Technology ascendant!

Fox, Warren Halsey. "Uncertain Future of Public Management." *Public*

Personnel Management 5 (July-August 1976):250-54. **Management effectiveness.**

Nothing new and nothing useful.

Lynn, Laurence E., Jr., and Seidl, John M. "'Bottom-Line' Management for Public Agencies." *Harvard Business Review* 55 (January-February 1977):144-53. **Management and controller roles.**

An article with a fascinating beginning that quickly slides into another management/control process prescription. This one is called CAMS (cooperative agency management system).

Marini, Frank, ed. *Toward a New Public Administration: The Minnowbrook Perspective.* Scranton, Pa.: Chandler Publishing, 1971. **Organization and management theory, Management models.**

A series of conference papers on the "new" public administration. As usual, there are a few bright spots in an otherwise dull collection.

Murray, Michael A. "Education for Public Administrators." *Public Personnel Management* 5 (July-August 1976):239. **Management education and training, Personnel management.**

Results of a mail survey conducted under the auspices of the National Association of Schools of Public Affairs and Administration (NASPAA).

Pressman, Jeffrey L., and Wildavsky, Aaron. *Implementation.* Berkeley: University of California Press, 1973. **Managerial effectiveness, Economic development.**

A unique study of project implementation—after the money is allocated and things have to get done. Although the study focuses on an economic development project in the U.S., the lessons are universal.

Schultze, Charles L. "The Public Use of Private Interest." *Harper's* 254 (May 1977):43-62. **Control systems and techniques, Evaluation and program effectiveness.**

A critique of the command-control orientation of federal programs and their evolution. The author advocates a market-like structure.

Steinhart, John H. "Wanted: Managers for the Public Sector." *European Business,* no. 40 (Winter-Spring 1974), pp. 51-56. **Management education and training.**

An examination of the transferability of private sector management expertise to the public sector. Some simplistic assumptions about private managers' abilities.

Yates, Douglas. "Making Decentralization Work: The View from City Hall." *Policy Sciences* 5 (1974):363-73. **Decentralization, Organization and management theory.**

A reasonable report of a New York effort to give neighborhoods more voice in city administration. No general lessons here, but informative nonetheless.

MANAGEMENT MODELS

Gonzalez, Richard F., and McMillan, Claude, Jr. "The Universality of American Management Philosophy." *Academy of Management Journal* 4 (April 1961):33-41. **Decision models, Developing countries.**

An unconvincing though interesting argument for the universality (read superiority) of "American" management; it is assumed to be scientific, systematic, orderly, and controlled.

Gorry, G. Anthony. "The Development of Managerial Models." *Sloan Management Review* 12 (Winter 1971):1-16. **Decisionmaking, Management policy, strategy, and style.**

A description of an effort to refine managerial models. The article is of little general utility. There is, however, an interesting concluding argument that calls for "experts" to interpret existing models.

Heller, Robert. *The Great Executive Dream.* New York: Delacorte, 1972. **Managerial functions, Organization and management theory.**

A light-hearted but not light-headed look at the many myths surrounding the work of managers and the practice of management.

Weiss, Alan J. "Surviving and Succeeding in the Political Organization." *Supervisory Management* 23 (May-September 1978). **Management policy, strategy, and style.**

A five-part series by a Kepner-Tregoe managing director that is full of advice. He has some interesting perspectives. For example: "Control means to restrain, govern, or otherwise dominate people and their behavior" (Part 3, July 1978, p. 21). This control is to be used to shape the organization *your* way.

MANAGEMENT POLICY, STRATEGY, AND STYLE

Bowman, James S. "The Behavioral Sciences: Fact and Fantasy in Organizations." *Personnel Journal* 55 (August 1976):395-97. **Management education and training, Analytical methods.**

An interesting survey of research on how behavioral sciences affect organizations. There is some evidence that organizational development, sensitivity training, job enrichment, etc. have had *no* impact.

Brown, Fred R., ed. *Management: Concepts and Practice.* 4th ed. Washington, D.C.: National Defense University, Industrial College of the Armed

Forces, 1976. **Control systems and techniques, Management in public organizations.**

An uneven collection of essays reflecting a highly formal view of how managers *should* behave. Subjects treated range from personnel management to international comparative management styles.

Brown, Lord Wilfred. "Give Managers a Chance to Manage." *International Management* 33 (September 1978):22-24. **Decisionmaking, Organization and management theory.**

A personal perspective on management, organizations, and objectives from a practicing manager who is also a management theorist.

Duncan, W. Jack. "Transferring Management Theory to Practice." *Academy of Management Journal* 17 (December 1974):724-38. **Organizational growth and change, Management education and training.**

The author assumes the efficacy of "management theory" and attributes "incalculable inefficiences" to skeptics, with no evidence for the assertion. There are some interesting data on how managers (skeptics?) and researchers rank linkage agents on innovation diffusion.

Hellriegel, Don, and Slocum, John. "Managerial Problem-Solving Styles." *Business Horizons* 18 (December 1975):29-37. **Managerial functions, Problem solving.**

A typology of management styles based on personality characteristics. Of little utility.

Hill, Roy. "The Relaxed Management Style of a High Technology Company." *International Management* 33 (March 1978):12-15. **Decentralization, Managerial functions.**

An interesting look at a corporate strategy that includes decentralization, duplication, and overlap. It works quite well.

Katz, Abraham. "There's No Room for Guesswork at IBM." *Planning Review* 5 (November 1977):3-9. **Control systems and techniques, Planning.**

Formal rationality, control, and planning are alive and well and ensconced in IBM. Fine in a non-competitive environment—but the future task environment for IBM appears highly competitive.

Keller, Robert T.; Slocum, John W., Jr.; and Susman, Gerald I. "Uncertainty and Type of Management System in Continuous Process Organizations." *Academy of Management Journal* 17 (March 1974):56-68. **Risk and uncertainty, Organization and management theory.**

A small survey (N = 44) of continuous process firms to ascertain type of management style in uncertain circumstances. Tedious, with some obvious conclusions.

McKenney, James L., and Keen, Peter G. W. "How Managers' Minds Work." *Harvard Business Review* 52 (May-June 1974):79-90. **Operations research and management science.**

A psychological profile of managers' cognitive styles. Some comparison is made with management scientists' approach to managing.

Mintzberg, Henry. "Policy as a Field of Management Theory." *Academy of Management Review* 2 (January 1977):88-103. **Management education and training.**

One of the best people in the field discusses policy and management education. An excellent article, with a significant (and useful) bibliography. **Highly recommended.**

Newman, Robert P., and Sussman, Lyle. "Controlling the Sycophant: Policies and Techniques of Corporation Presidents." *SAM Advanced Management Journal* 43 (Autumn 1978):14-21. **Information management, Managerial functions.**

A reasonably good report on a small survey (N = 26) of chief executive officers' efforts to gather reliable information.

Stout, Russell, Jr. *Management or Control? The Organizational Challenge.* Bloomington: Indiana University Press, 1980. **Manager and controller roles, Managerial functions.**

A detailed argument for clearer theoretical and practical distinctions between management and control. Too much reliance on control as a model for organizational action produces problems that could be avoided. **Recommended.**

Truell, George F. "Core Managerial Strategies Culled from Behavioral Research." *Supervisory Management* 22 (January 1977):10-17. **Management effectiveness.**

A shopping list of various approaches to personnel motivation. The author outlines ten "central principles" of the more popular techniques and methods.

Tsaklanganos, Angelos A. "Peers, Persuasion, and Horizontal Management." *Management Accounting* 60 (August 1978):33-37. **Organizational communication, Decentralization.**

The provocative beginnings of an argument for horizontal organization, but it is not developed enough to be of much use.

Vancil, Richard F. "Strategy Formulation in Complex Organizations."

Sloan Management Review 16 (Winter 1975):1-18. **Organizational goals and objectives, Organization and management theory.**

Avoid. This article is of little use to scholar or practitioner.

MANAGER AND CONTROLLER ROLES

Anderson, William J. "Management Control: The Uncertain Role of Internal Audit." *Government Accountants Journal* 26 (Summer 1977):15-19. **Control systems and techniques, Auditing.**

The internal audit's role in control. This is interesting because it was written by a GAO auditor.

Argentima, John. "And Now for the New Masters." *Accountancy* 88 (January 1977):94-99. **Accounting, Organization and management theory.**

A British accountant's view of the future of management and the new role of accounting. This is a good, hard analysis of real trends in management and accounting.

Beard, Donald W. "The Effects of Organizational Size and Complexity on Managerial Role Structure: An Exploratory Analysis." *Academy of Management Proceedings* 38 (August 1978):170-74. **Organizational design, Organizational structure.**

A statistical analysis of the managerial role in various industrial organizations. The discussion is muddled and inconclusive.

Day, Charles R., Jr. "Management's Mindless Mistakes." *Industry Week* (29 May 1978), pp. 34-42. **Management policy, strategy, and style, Error detection and correction.**

An interesting anecdotal account of some managerial goofs, with no suggestions on how they might be avoided beyond the usual "consider people."

Frohman, Alan L. "The Performance of Innovation: Managerial Roles." *California Management Review* 20 (Spring 1978):5-12. **Research and development, Innovation.**

A lightweight piece that takes another look at the manager's impact on innovations, this time in R&D organizations.

Laurent, André. "Managerial Subordinacy: A Neglected Aspect of Organizational Hierarchies." *Academy of Management Review* 3 (April 1978):220-30. **Hierarchy, Organization and management theory.**

An examination of the literature on hierarchic roles. This is an inconclusive piece, with some suggestions for further research.

Lawrence, Paul R.; Kolodny, Harvey F.; and Davis, Stanley M. "The Human Side of the Matrix." *Organizational Dynamics* 6 (Summer 1977):43-61. **Organizational structure, Organization and management theory.**

An excellent primer on the concept and structure of matrix organization. **Recommended.**

McMahon, J. Timothy, and Ivancevich, John M. "A Study of Control in a Manufacturing Organization: Managers and Nonmanagers." *Administrative Science Quarterly* 21 (March 1976):66-83. **Control systems and techniques, Organization and management theory.**

A study of the varying perceptions of control in organizations. There are some interesting findings, but the presentation is needlessly complicated and obscure.

MANAGERIAL FUNCTIONS

Barnard, Chester I. *The Functions of the Executive.* Cambridge, Mass.: Harvard University Press, 1968. **Organization and management theory.**

A classic that must be read by all interested in organization and management. Barnard brought a lifetime of experience to bear on the question of what managers (or executives) do that differentiates them from other organizational members. **Recommended.**

Braybrooke, David. "The Mystery of Executive Success Re-examined." *Administrative Science Quarterly* 8 (March 1964):533-60. **Management policy, strategy, and style, Organization and management theory.**

A brilliant essay on what constitutes executive success. This article provides both an explanation and an agenda for research. **Highly recommended.**

Campbell, John P. et al. *Managerial Behavior, Performance, and Effectiveness.* New York: McGraw-Hill, 1970. **Management effectiveness, Organization and management theory.**

A rather formal attempt at managerial assessment, this volume is not as useful as the empirical studies (see Mintzberg, Sayles, and Woodward, for example).

Cleverley, Graham. *Managers and Magic.* New York: E. P. Dutton, 1973. **Analytical methods, Organization and management theory.**

An original work that examines the various functions of management methods and practices. The author compares them with the magical activities of so-called primitive societies.

Cummings, Larry L.; Hinton, Bernard L.; and Gobdel, Bruce C. "Creative Behavior as a Function of Task Environment: Impact of Objectives, Procedures and Controls." *Academy of Management Journal* 18 (September 1975):489-99. **Management effectiveness, Control systems and techniques.**

An examination of the effects of various control strategies on creative performance. The authors question broad interpretations of how task environment influences creativity.

Dew, R. B., and Gee, K. P. "Managements' Use of Budgetary Information." *Management Accounting* 48 (March 1970):89-92. **Information management, Budgeting.**

One of a series of empirical studies conducted by the authors. The concern is always with the actual use of information, not just processing, storage, or retrieval.

————. "Frequency of Performance Reporting and Managers Reference for Control: A Note." *Accounting and Business Research,* no. 7 (Summer 1972), pp. 234-36. **Information management, Control systems and techniques.**

Another of the Dew and Gee reports. This one is short but still worthwhile, since the focus is on *use.*

Diebold Group. *Rethinking the Practice of Management.* New York: Praeger, 1973. **Organization and management theory.**

Not so much rethinking as relabeling. This is another formal exercise that does little to add to our understanding of management practices.

Drucker, Peter F. *The Practice of Management.* New York: Harper and Row, 1954. **Management policy, strategy, and style, Organization and management theory.**

In one of his early works, Drucker examines the nature of management, with an emphasis on improving individual and organizational productivity. Examples are drawn from major U.S. corporations.

————. *Management: Tasks, Responsibilities, Practices.* New York: Harper and Row, 1974. **Management policy, strategy, and style, Organization and management theory.**

This book has received a great deal of attention, but it may be like *War and Peace*—not many people read it. Drucker is interested in management, and his work merits attention since that interest is informed and useful. This is an important reference work.

Grey, Ronald J., and Gordon, George G. "Risk-Taking Managers: Who Gets the Top Jobs?" *Management Review* 67 (November 1978):9-13. **Decisionmaking, Risk and uncertainty.**

A shallow substantiation of managers as risk-takers.

Higgins, Richard B. "Managerial Behavior in Upwardly Oriented Organizations." *California Management Review* 14 (Spring 1972):49-59. **Participative management, Management effectiveness.**

This article is a study of how leadership, "followership," and decentralization combine for a good fit between organization, tasks, and people.

Hunsicker, Frank R. "What Successful Managers Say About Their Skills." *Personnel Journal* 57 (November 1978):618-21. **Management effectiveness, Management education and training.**

An interesting self-appraisal of management skills by managers. Using military managers as subjects may prompt questioning their representativeness, but the author finds the responses consistent with other studies.

Koontz, Harold. *Appraising Managers as Managers.* New York: McGraw-Hill, 1971. **Management effectiveness, Manager and controller roles.**

An outline of how managers might be evaluated and assessed. The author views management as a cybernetic control exercise and recommends MBO as an appraisal system.

————, and O'Donnell, Cyril. *Principles of Management: An Analysis of Managerial Functions.* 4th ed. New York: McGraw-Hill, 1968. **Management history, Organization and management theory.**

A text that illustrates how the early "principles" live on. All you have to do is believe.

Landau, Martin, and Stout, Russell, Jr. "To Manage Is Not to Control: Or the Folly of Type II Errors." *Public Administration Review* 39 (March-April 1979):148-56. **Management control, Organization and management theory.**

A distinction is made between the concepts of management and control. This is the first effort to deal with the practical implications each has for organizations. **Recommended.**

Mintzberg, Henry. *The Nature of Managerial Work.* New York: Harper and Row, 1973. **Organization and management theory.**

One of the very few systematic empirical studies of managers' *work*—not principles and prescriptions, but what managers do. **Highly recommended.**

————. "A New Look at the Chief Executive's Job." *Organizational Dynamics* 1 (Winter 1973):20-30. **Management policy, strategy, and style, Organization and management theory.**

An excellent empirical examination of the *practice* of managing. **Highly recommended.**

Muse, William V. "The Universality of Management." *Academy of Management Journal* 10 (June 1967):179-84. **Organization and management theory.**

A shallow examination of management principles. This is not much help to anyone.

Sapolsky, Harvey M. *The Polaris System Development: Bureaucratic and Programmatic Success in Government.* Cambridge, Mass.: Harvard University Press, 1972. **Research and development, PERT and CPM.**

In a splendid empirical study of the Polaris submarine development program, Sapolsky has produced a masterful analysis of how organizations *really* get things done in uncertain circumstances. **Highly recommended.**

Sayles, Leonard R., *Managerial Behavior: Administration in Complex Organizations.* New York: McGraw-Hill, 1964. **Organization and management theory, Organizational performance.**

An example of Sayles's early work. The concern with *actual* managerial behavior is what distinguishes material like this from platitudinous principles.

————, and Chandler, Margaret K. *Managing Large Systems: Organizations for the Future.* New York: Harper and Row, 1971. **Organizational growth and change, Research and development.**

Probably the definitive study of the U.S. National Aeronautics and Space Administration (NASA). The authors have made organizational and theoretical sense of a highly complex R&D, technological, and political agency. **Highly recommended.**

Simon, Leonard S.; Lamar, Charles; and Haines, George H., Jr. "Manager's Uses of Models." *Omega* 4 (1976):253-64. **Management models, Organizational goals and objectives.**

A discussion of models used to describe managers' behavior. This is a sensible presentation, illustrating how "hidden goals" shape alternatives to the formal decision model.

Skinner, Wickham, and Sasser, W. Earl. "Managers with Impact: Versatile and Inconsistent." *Harvard Business Review* 55 (November-December 1977):140-48. **Management policy, strategy, and style.**

The authors found some interesting things about the practice of managing, but wind up saying that managers succeed by succeeding.

Sloma, Richard S. *No-Nonsense Management.* New York: Macmillan, 1977.

A non-book. Don't waste your time or money.

Stewart, Rosemary. *Managers and Their Jobs: A Study of the Similarities and Differences in the Ways Managers Spend Their Time.* London: Macmillan, 1967. **Organization and management theory.**

With Mintzberg and Sayles, Stewart is one of the few researchers studying *what* managers do and *how* they go about doing it. This study was done in Britain, but shows commonality with later studies done elsewhere. **Recommended.**

————. *How Computers Affect Management.* London: Macmillan, 1971. **Organization and management theory, Computer services.**

Stewart continues her fine efforts at investigating managerial *work.* This study gets beyond alarmist doom-saying and Panglossian hardware-pushing. **Recommended.**

——-. "To Understand the Manager's Job: Consider Demands, Constraints, Choices." *Organization Dynamics* 4 (Spring 1976):22-32. **Management education and training.**

An excellent research report on what managers do—in contrast to what we think they should do. **Recommended.**

Stuart, Alexander. "U.S. Home's Management Religion." *Fortune* 98 (4 December 1978):66. **Management policy, strategy, and style, Management effectiveness, Organizational design.**

A short outline of corporate rebuilding by a "super-manager." There are some interesting observations on links between theory and corporate experiences and how an organization can be turned into a winner after being labeled a loser.

Tarrant, John J. *Drucker: The Man Who Invented the Corporate Society.* Boston: Cahners Books, 1976. **Management history, Organization and management theory.**

An excellent biography and analysis of Drucker's ideas and their influence on mainstream management education and consulting. **Recommended.**

Thain, Donald H. "The Ideal General Manager." *Business Quarterly* 43 (Summer 1978):75-81. **Organization and management theory.**

An attempt to outline the ideal manager's characteristics. I am not quite sure what purpose such exercises are intended to serve. What properties are most/least important?

————. "The Functions of the General Manager." *Business Quarterly* 43 (Autumn 1978):53-61. **Organization and management theory.**

Another shopping list of "how to be a successful manager."

"The New Planning." *Business Week,* no. 2565 (18 December 1978), p. 62. **Planning, Decisionmaking.**

This is not very analytic, but it does provide a view of corporate executives as opportunistic, entrepreneurial planners who are not locked in to set procedures.

Vinci, Vincent. "Can a Good Manager Manage Anything?" *Administrative Management* 37 (September 1976):65. **Management effectiveness, Management education and training.**

A trivial listing of the characteristics of a "good" manager. Not much help is given, but at least the author acknowledges our ignorance in this realm.

Woodward, Joan. *Management and Technology.* London: Her Majesty's Stationary Office, 1959. **Organization and management theory, Organizational effectiveness.**

A classic work, this is one of the earliest efforts to empirically examine the meaning of organizational structure, technological change, and management. **Recommended.**

Zaleznik, Abraham. "Managers and Leaders: Are They Different?" *Harvard Business Review* 55 (May-June 1977):67-78. **Management education and training.**

An interesting distinction is made between managers who maintain stability and leaders who create new approaches. Development of one characteristic may be inimical to the other.

PARTICIPATIVE MANAGEMENT

Steinmetz, Lawrence L., and Greenidge, Charles D. "Realities That Shape Managerial Style." *Business Horizons* 13 (October 1970):23-32. **Managerial functions.**

An intelligent look at the prevailing myths of participative management. There is now evidence to support the authors' early skepticism. See Thorsrud's "Democracy at Work."

Thimm, Alfred L. "Decision-Making at Volkswagen 1972-1975." *Columbia Journal of World Business* 2 (Spring 1976):94-103. **Decisionmaking, Organizational growth and change.**

A good analysis of corporate decisionmaking and the interplay of public policy and private firms.

Thorsrud, Einar. "Democracy at Work: Norwegian Experiences with Non-Bureaucratic Forms of Organization." *Journal of Applied Behavioral Science* 13 (July-September 1977):410-21. **Management policy, strategy, and style, Organizational design.**

A report on participative management in Norway. There are instructive lessons for those interested in undertaking similar strategies—it's not easy.

PERSONNEL MANAGEMENT

Acker, Joan, and van Houten, Donald R. "Differential Recruitment and Control: The Sex Structuring of Organizations." *Administrative Science Quarterly* 19 (June 1974):152-63. **Organizational behavior.**

One of the rare systematic examinations of this issue. Despite popular interest, there is little research into sex structuring in organizations. Researchers take note.

Archer, Earnest R. "The Myth of Motivation." *Personnel Administrator* 23 (December 1978):57-65. **Organizational psychology, Organization and management theory.**

A rather confused discussion with too much jargon and too many undefined concepts.

Golembiewski, Robert T., and Proehl, Carl W., Jr. "A Survey of the Empirical Literature on Flexible Work Hours: Character and Consequence of a Major Innovation." *Academy of Management Review* 3 (October 1978):837-53. **Organizational psychology, Performance appraisal.**

A much-needed survey of experiences with flexi-time. **Recommended.**

Holt, H. O., and Stevenson, F. L. "Human Performance Considerations in Complex Systems." *Journal of Systems Management* 29 (October 1978):14-20. **Computer services.**

Handling the man-machine "interface." The author presents some problems in "human factors engineering" and computer-based systems.

Walker, James W. "Manpower Planning: How Is It Really Applied?" *European Business*, no. 39 (Winter 1973), pp. 72-78. **Managerial functions.**

A report of the status of manpower planning in U.S. and European businesses. This is more an exhortation than a research study.

PROJECT MANAGEMENT

Maciariello, Joseph A. "Making Program Management Work, Part 1." *Journal of Systems Management* 25 (June 1974):8-15. "Part 2." 25 (July 1974):20-27. **Organizational control, Organizational learning.**

Another hyper-control statement. The author ignores practically all that is known about organizational behavior.

Maieli, Vincent. "Management by Hindsight: Diary of a Project Manager." *Management Review* (June 1971), pp. 4-14. **Research and development, Control systems and techniques.**

A fictitious diary of an industrial project manager's experience. The journal editors comment that it illustrates the need for a project manager to be in control. But if things are in control, who needs a project manager?

Meek, Richard L. "Project Selection in the Petroleum Industry." *Research Management* 14 (September 1971):62-67. **Research and development, Analytical methods.**

Petroleum industry project selection is not guided by formal, academic methods, according to the author.

Miller, William B. "Fundamentals of Project Management." *Journal of Systems Management* 29 (November 1978):22-29. **Planning, Control systems and techniques.**

Project management as a closed system activity—with a checklist yet. But there is no discussion of personnel or environmental considerations.

Rolefson, Jerome F. "Project Management: Six Critical Steps." *Journal of Systems Management* 29 (April 1978):10-17. **Organizational effectiveness, Planning.**

Formalistic gibberish.

SCIENTIFIC MANAGEMENT

Fry, Louis W. "The Maligned F. W. Taylor: A Reply to His Many Critics." *Academy of Managment Review* 1 (July 1976):124-29. **Operations research and management science, Organization and management theory.**

In this shallow reply, the author does not deal with some of the more telling criticisms of Taylor. Some interesting information on time-study abuses.

Taylor, F. W. *Hearings Before Special Committee of the House of Representatives to Investigate the Taylor and Other Systems of Shop Management under Authority of House Resolution 90.* Washington, D.C.: U.S. Government Printing Office, 1912. **Management history, Managerial functions.**

Taylor's testimony provides the best perspective on his own interpretation of the impact and utility of his work. It may be hard to get, but it is worth the effort for the serious student of management practices.

―――. *The Principles of Scientific Management.* New York: W. W. Norton, 1967. **Management history, Managerial functions.**

A classic; the definitive work on the subject. This is the book that started a movement and must be read to appreciate modern organizational history. There is now some dispute over Taylor's claim to sole authorship. See Wrege and Stotka, "Cooke Creates a Classic." *Academy of Management Review* 3 (October 1978):736-49. **Recommended.**

Organization

ADMINISTRATIVE REFORM

Brown, David S. "The Myth of Reorganizing." *Journal of Systems Management* 30 (June 1979):6-10. **Management policy, strategy, and style, Organization and management theory.**

A brief rehash of the perils of reorganization. This is a good, easy-to-read statement.

Maggin, Donald L. "How Carter Reorganized the EOP." *Management Review* (May 1978), pp. 11-17. **Decisionmaking, Organizational design.**

Of some historical interest. A view of a member of the project staff that prepared the EOP reorganization plan. How successful are these "reforms"?

Malek, Frederic V. "Management Improvement in the Federal Government." *Business Horizons* 14 (August 1971):11-17. **Manager and controller roles, Management in public organizations.**

A presidential assistant's account of how federal management was improved in 1971. It must have been a temporary measure.

Rosen, Gerald R. "Is Civil Service Outmoded?" *Dun's Review* 110 (November 1977):46-50. **Organizational effectiveness, Management in public organizations.**

A capsule history of past and current efforts at civil service reform. The lack of a profit-loss measure is brought up again, but even with the editorializing it's worth a look.

Warwick, Donald P. *A Theory of Public Bureaucracy.* Cambridge, Mass.: Harvard University Press, 1975. **Bureaucracy, Organization and managment theory.**

An empirical study of reform and reorganization in the U.S. State Department. In this insightful work, the author makes some interesting recommendations.

BOUNDARY SPANNING

Aldrich, Howard, and Herker, Diane. "Boundary Spanning Roles and Organization Structure." *Academy of Management Journal* 2 (April 1977):217-30. **Organizational structure, Organization and management theory.**

A good explication of boundary-spanning roles in and across formal organization. There is no empirical content, but the authors give excellent suggestions for further investigation.

Callahan, Robert, and Salipante, Paul, Jr. "Boundary Spanning Units: Organizational Implications for the Management of Innovation." *Human Resource Management* 18 (Spring 1979):26-31. **Innovation, Management policy, strategy, and style.**

A good statement on establishing a temporary organizational unit to deal with uncertainty. The new unit buffered more certain activities, but it was not disruptive because it was temporary.

Keller, Robert T. "Boundary-Spanning Activity, Role Dynamics, and Job Satisfaction: A Longitudinal Study." *Journal of Business Research* 6 (May 1978):147-58. **Personnel management, Organizational conflict.**

A study of boundary spanning and its effects on role conflict ambiguity and job satisfaction. The effects were found to be contrary to former hypothesized relationships. Boundary spanning did not increase conflict.

Leifer, Richard, and Delbecq, André. "Organizational/Environmental Interchange: A Model of Boundary Spanning Activity." *Academy of Management Review* 3 (January 1978):40-50. **Organization and management theory, Decision analysis.**

A restatement of most of the work in this area. Nothing new, but useful as a primer if the terms are unfamiliar.

Organ, Dennis W. "Linking Pins Between Organizations and Environment." *Business Horizons* 14 (December 1971):73-80. **Organizational effectiveness, Manager and controller roles.**

The author re-labels boundary spanners as "boundary agents." No reason is given.

Swanson, Burton E. *Organizing Agricultural Technology Transfer.* Bloomington: PASITAM, Indiana University, 1975; and *Regional Ag-*

ricultural Production Programs: Training and Design Strategies. Bloomington: PASITAM, Indiana University, 1976. **Research and development, Developing countries.**

Two good, short books reporting the results of a study of IRRI (International Rice Research Institute) and CIMMYT (International Maize and Wheat Improvement Center) and the effects of organizational design, management practices, and training on their activities.

BUREAUCRACY

Bennis, Warren G. "Organizational Developments and the Fate of Bureaucracy." *Industrial Management Review* 7 (1966):41-55. **Organization and management theory, Organizational growth and change.**

The now-classic piece that predicted "the end of bureaucracy" in the 25-50 years from 1964. The author has since modified this view.

―――. "A Funny Thing Happened on the Way to the Future." *American Psychologist* 25 (July 1970):595-608. **Organizational growth and change, Organization and management theory.**

Reflecting on his 1966 article, the author updates his earlier pronouncement on society and organizations.

Cohen, Harry. *The Demonics of Bureaucracy.* Ames: Iowa State University Press, 1965. **Organizational behavior, Organization and management theory.**

Bureaucracy from the inside. Cohen presents a sociological study, based on his experiences as an employee in a governmental agency. This is a refinement and update of findings in a similar study carried out in the 1940s, with some interesting empirical evidence to support sociological thinking of the 1940s and 1950s.

Elgin, Duane S., and Bushnell, Robert A. "The Limits to Complexity: Are Bureaucracies Becoming Unmanageable?" *The Futurist* 11 (December 1977):337-49. **Organization and management theory.**

An institutional "limits to growth" argument. The authors make some good points, but they are bound by a formal model of corporate efficiency for public organizations.

Hlavacek, James D., and Thompson, Victor A. "Bureaucracy and New Product Innovation." *Academy of Management Journal* 16 (September 1973):361-72. **Innovation.**

A report of a study that identifies a trend away from formal bureaucratic organization in new product development and the formation of "venture groups."

Merton, Robert K. et al., eds. *Reader in Bureaucracy.* New York: Free Press, 1952. **Organization and management theory, Management history.**

A marvelous collection. This is quite possibly the best set of readings on the subject. The editors have selected essays from Weber, Michels, Thorstein Veblen, Herbert Simon, Merton, and others to make this a unique book. **Recommended.**

Reimann, Bernard D. "On the Dimensions of Bureaucratic Structure: An Empirical Reappraisal." *Administrative Science Quarterly* 18 (1973): 462-76. **Organizational structure, Organization and management theory.**

A short examination of a classic bureaucratic model. The author recommends a concept of multidimensional structure space—an unspecified (and perhaps unspecifiable) form.

Steiner, John F., and Edmunds, Stahrl W. "Ascientific Beliefs About Large Organizations and Adaptation to Change." *Academy of Management Review* 4 (1979):107-12.

A sweeping oversimplification of "prelogical" views of society and organization. The article does make some intriguing points, but it is much too short to properly develop them.

Wilson, James Q., and Rachal, Patricia. "Can the Government Regulate Itself?" *Public Interest,* no. 46 (Winter 1977), pp. 3-14. **Management in public organizations.**

The issue of accountability, size, and authority in federal agencies. The journal is considered a sounding board for social critics and "neo-conservative" intellectuals.

DECENTRALIZATION

Peltu, Malcolm. "End of an Era for Giant Computers." *International Management* 34 (June 1979):33-35. **Computer services, Information processing.**

A short report on the advantages and disadvantages of centralization and the centralizing tendencies of data processing services.

Perrow, Charles. "The Bureaucratic Paradox: The Efficient Organization Centralizes in Order to Decentralize." *Organizational Dynamics* 5 (Spring 1977):3-14. **Organizational effectiveness, Decisionmaking.**

This reads like a "think-piece" for a book. Perrow's ideas are not fully developed, and a potentially valuable exploration goes begging. A good article, though.

Sullivan, Dale B. "Task Environments and Organization Structure." *Organization and Administrative Sciences* 8 (Summer-Fall 1977):185-200. **Organizational structure, Decisionmaking.**

An interesting study of the influence of task environment and decentralization on organizational decisionmaking.

"What Undid Jarman: Paperwork Paralysis." *Business Week,* no. 2467 (24 January 1977), pp. 67-68. **Manager and controller roles, Control systems and techniques.**

A short account of what happened to a control-happy chief executive officer. Interesting lesson.

Yates, Douglas. "Making Decentralization Work: The View from City Hall." *Policy Sciences* 5 (1974):363-73. **Organizational learning, Policy analysis.**

A report on the neighborhood government experiment in New York, under John Lindsey's administration. There are some important lessons in the *attempt,* though it did not succeed.

HIERARCHY

Evans, Peter B. "Multiple Hierarchies and Organizational Control." *Administrative Science Quarterly* 20 (June 1975):250-59. **Organizational control, Organization and management theory.**

The author recognizes the problems of hierarchy and control (compliance), but he argues that a dual hierarchy is the answer. Curious.

Lauterburg, Christoph. "Why Hierarchies Are Superfluous." *International Management* 34 (June 1979):45-46. **Organization and management theory, Organizational communication, Organizational design.**

A very brief but informative statement on the character and problems of hierarchy. The author uses some empirical referents to support his assertions.

INNOVATION

Abernathy, William J., and Chakravarthy, Balaji S. "Government Intervention and Innovation in Industry: A Policy Framework." *Sloan Management Review* 20 (Spring 1979):3-18. **Organizational behavior, Policy analysis.**

A "conceptual framework" is offered to aid in understanding the interplay of government and industry in developing and implementing innovations.

Parker, R. C. "How Managements Innovate." *Management Today* (September 1978), p. 43. **Organizational design, Comparative management. management.**

A report on the first stage of a study on how corporate innovations are generated and handled in the U.K. The firms examined are not necessarily typical of British industry; therefore, Parker's findings are questionable.

Quinn, James Brian. "Technological Innovation, Entrepreneurship, and Strategy." *Sloan Management Review* 20 (Spring 1979):19-30. **Management policy, strategy, and style, Managerial functions.**

An outline of how to encourage innovation and entrepreneurial behavior in large-scale organizations.

Sapolsky, Harvey M. "Organizational Structure and Innovation." *Journal of Business* 40 (1967):497-510. **Organizational structure, Organization and management theory.**

A study of innovation and implications for organizational design, based on data gathered from retail department stores.

Udell, Gerald G.; Baker, Ken; and Colton, Robert M. "Stimulating and Rewarding Invention: The Innovation Center Program." *Research Management* 22 (July 1978):32-38. **Management education and training, Managerial functions.**

Report of a long-term university-centered effort to assist and train inventors and entrepreneurs. The program bears watching.

Warner, Kenneth E. "The Need for Some Innovative Concepts of Innovation: An Examination of Research on the Diffusion of Innovations." *Policy Sciences* 5 (1974):433-51. **Organizational behavior, Organizational learning.**

A survey article. The author notes that the failure of innovations has been the subject of adequate research.

Zaltman, Gerald; Duncan, Robert; and Holbek, Jonny. *Innovations and Organizations*. New York: John Wiley, 1973. **Bureaucracy, Organizational structure.**

A literature survey on innovation in organization. This is a short, sensible work, with a good bibliography and index—not all that common in works of this type.

ORGANIZATION AND MANAGEMENT THEORY

Arrow, Kenneth J. *The Limits of Organization*. New York: W.W. Norton, 1974. **Economic analysis, Organizational goals and objectives.**

A brilliant essay by one of the world's foremost economists and thinkers. Arrow takes a penetrating look at the individual, society, and organizations. **Recommended.**

Baltz, Gerald W. "A Practical Application of Management and Organization Theory for the Academic Administration." *Academy of Management Review* 1 (July 1976):129-33. **Organizational growth and change, Contingency theory.**

A simplistic outline of "classic" organization and management theory for academic application. This is a good example of a failure to learn from experience.

Barthol, Richard P. "The Placebo Organization." *California Management Review* 20 (Summer 1978):26-30. **Organizational design, Organizational growth and change.**

A tongue-in-cheek examination of academic organization theory and organization functions. Fun, with the bite of truth.

Beer, Stafford. *Brain of the Firm.* New York: Herder and Herder, 1972. **Operations research and management science, Control systems and techniques.**

A brilliant exposition on the cybernetic model of the firm. Terms and concepts are clarified, discussed, and applied to management problems. Beer is one of those people who must be heeded, whether you agree with him or not. **Recommended.**

Behling, Orlando. "Some Problems in the Philosophy of Science of Organizations." *Academy of Management Review* 3 (April 1978):193-201. **Analytical methods, Systems theory.**

A useful survey of various theories of organization and management. This is a sensible, though not particularly insightful, critique.

Blois, K. J. "Problems in Applying Organizational Theory to Industrial Marketing." *Industrial Marketing Management* 6 (1977):273-80. **Organizational learning.**

An overly ambitious title and not much content.

Boguslaw, Robert. *The New Utopians.* Englewood Cliffs, N.J.: Prentice-Hall, 1965. **Systems analysis, Analytical methods.**

An excellent critique of the modern quest for the analytic utopia. This is an intelligent, measured effort that goes beyond polemic to raise some very important questions. **Recommended.**

Child, John. "Strategies of Control and Organizational Behavior." *Administrative Science Quarterly* 18 (March 1973):1-17. **Decentralization, Control systems and techniques.**

A tedious study. There are, however, some interesting data on organizational structure and behavior.

Cooper, W. W.; Leavitt, H. J.; and Shelly, M. W., II, eds. *New Perspectives in Organization Research.* New York: John Wiley, 1964. **Organizational effectiveness, Organizational structure.**

A good collection of essays and research suggestions that is still as timely and useful as when first published. This volume can still serve as a comprehensive introduction to different views of organizations, management, and control. **Recommended.**

Cyert, Richard M., and March, James G. *A Behavioral Theory of the Firm.* Englewood Cliffs, N.J.: Prentice-Hall, 1963. **Managerial functions.**

A classic, this is the seminal work that prompted a drastic reconsideration of the organization and management of the firm. **Recommended.**

Dewar, Robert, and Hage, Jerald. "Size, Technology, Complexity, and Structural Differentiation: Toward a Theoretical Synthesis." *Administrative Science Quarterly* 23 (March 1978):111-36. **Organizational design, Organizational structure.**

A modest attempt to point the way toward better informed empirical research into the complexities of organizational processes. A good argument against the theoretical and methodological errors of most research.

Emery, Fred E. "Bureaucracy and Beyond." *Organizational Dynamics* 3 (Winter 1974):3-13. **Bureaucracy, Organizational design.**

A rather superficial discussion of work and the work-place in classical and modern theories of management and organization.

Evan, William M. "Organization Theory and Organizational Effectiveness: An Exploratory Analysis." *Organization and Administrative Sciences* 7 (Spring-Summer 1976):15-28. **Systems analysis, Organizational effectiveness.**

Another literature review of some academic interest.

Fayol, Henri. *Administration industrielle et générale.* Paris, 1916 and 1925. English translation by J. A. Coubrough (Geneva, 1930) and Constance Storrs (London: Pitman, 1949). **Management history, Managerial functions.**

The classic statement on management principles. **Recommended.**

Filley, Alan C.; House, Robert J.; and Kerr, Steven. *Managerial Process and Organizational Behavior.* 2d ed. Glenview, Ill.: Scott, Foresman, 1976. **Managerial functions, Organizational behavior.**

An excellent text whose elements are well-organized and lucid. There are name and subject indexes and an extensive bibliography. **Highly recommended.**

Flippo, Edwin B., and Munsinger, Gary M. *Management.* 3d ed. Boston: Allyn and Bacon, 1975. **Managerial functions, Organizational behavior.**

Another text—undistinguished, but adequate.

Gadalla, Ibrahim E., and Cooper, Robert. "Towards an Epistemology of Management." *Social Science Information* 17 (1978):349-83. **Management history.**

A tedious, wordy exposition on the cultural context of organization and management theory. Most of this has been said before—and more simply.

Gerth, H. H., and Mills, C. Wright, trans., eds. *From Max Weber: Essays in Sociology.* New York: Oxford University Press, 1946. **Bureaucracy, Comparative management.**

Modern bureaucratic organizations cannot be understood and appreciated without reading Weber. This is the most accessible and readable translation of essays from his major works. **Recommended.**

Gorelik, George. "On Some Measures of Organization." *Organization and Administrative Sciences* 8 (Winter 1977-78):35-43. **Organizational structure.**

A technical, mathematical examination of the general concept of organization and entropy.

Gribbins, Ronald E., and Hunt, Shelby D. "Is Management a Science?" *Academy of Management Review* 3 (January 1978):139-44. **Operations research and management science.**

A conceptual note. Some good points are raised, but on the whole this is a trivial piece. The authors do little to answer the question, largely because they ignore the hypothetical element of science and management.

Gulick, L., and Urwick, L., eds. *Papers on the Science of Administration.* New York: Institute of Public Administration, Columbia University, 1937. **Management history, Managerial functions.**

Probably the earliest attempt (in English) to provide a fully articulated set of principles for organizing, managing, and controlling large formal organizations. The influence of this collection is beyond measure. **Recommended.**

Hirschman, Albert O. *Exit, Voice, and Loyalty: Responses to Decline in Firms, Organizations, and States.* Cambridge, Mass.: Harvard University Press, 1970. **Economic analysis, Organizational effectiveness.**

A brilliant book by one of the most perceptive thinkers in political/economic theory. Hirschman's work provides an understanding of many of the problems facing organizations and society.

Hood, Christopher C. *The Limits of Administration.* London: John Wiley, 1976. **Organizational growth and change, Organizational design.**

The book moves from a model of "perfect" administration to a more realistic organizational condition. Chapter 7 on administrative control is particularly insightful.

Keller, Robert T. "A Look at the Sociotechnical System." *California Management Review* 15 (Fall 1972):86-91. **Organizational effectiveness, Organizational design.**

Another literature review, with a modest proposal on technical considerations and organizational size.

Landau, Martin. *Political Theory and Political Science.* New York: Macmillan, 1972. **Policy analysis.**

An unfortunate title that masks what is one of the most intelligent and original works on politics and organization. **Highly recommended.**

————. "Federalism, Redundancy and System Reliability." *Publius* 3 (Fall 1973):173-96. **Redundancy, Organizational learning.**

An interesting discussion of organization and government reliability and how it can be enhanced by the judicious use of redundant forms. The example used is the federal structure of the U.S. government.

Lev, Baruch. "Environmental Uncertainty Reduction by Smoothing and Buffering: An Empirical Verification." *Academy of Management Journal* 18 (December 1975):864-71. **Decisionmaking, Risk and uncertainty.**

An interesting academic examination of the buffering and smoothing propositions of organization and management theory. Technical, but worth a look.

Magnusen, Karl O. "A Comparative Analysis of Organizations: A Critical Review." *Organizational Dynamics* (Summer 1973), pp. 16-31. **Organizational behavior.**

A review and critique of mainstream organization and management theory. Nothing new.

Mansfield, Roger. "Bureaucracy and Centralization: An Examination of Organizational Structure." *Administrative Science Quarterly* 18 (December 1973):477-88. **Bureaucracy, Decentralization.**

An empirical/statistical examination of Max Weber's "ideal type" bureaucracy. Quite properly, the authors use the Weberian model as a basis for comparative analysis.

March, James G., ed. *Handbook of Organizations*. Chicago: Rand McNally, 1965. **Management history.**

A superlative collection. If you own only one book on organizations, this is the one to have. **Highly recommended.**

————, and Simon, Herbert A. *Organizations*. New York: John Wiley, 1958. **Management history.**

A classic still in print in the 1970s—and well it should be. This is an essential volume in a basic library of organizational works. **Recommended.**

Murray, Michael A. "Modern Management Applied to Academic Decisions." *Academy of Management Review* 1 (January 1976):79-88. **Decisionmaking, Management accounting.**

An excellent example of an uncritical acceptance of a technique's effectiveness in one domain while questioning its applicability in another. The author shows a mistaken understanding of decisionmaking contexts and the scientific method.

Mouzelis, Nicos P. *Organization and Bureaucracy*. Chicago: Aldine, 1967. **Management history, Bureaucracy.**

A good summary and analysis of most of the main elements of organization and management theory and practice.

Perrow, Charles. "The Short and Glorious History of Organizational Theory." *Organizational Dynamics* 2 (Summer 1973):2-15. **Management history.**

A free and easy review. Highly readable, with sensible, cautious conclusions.

Pugh, D. S., ed. *Organization Theory: Selected Readings*. Baltimore: Penguin, 1971. **Management history.**

A good introductory set of readings. Most of the major contributors to modern organization and management theory are represented. **Highly recommended.**

Reinharth, Leon. "The Missing Ingredient in Organization Theory." *SAM Advanced Management Journal* (Winter 1978), pp. 14-24. **Managerial functions.**

The author proposes that "key leadership" is the missing element in classic organization and management theory. It's difficult, however, to understand what the concept means.

Robbins, Stephen P. "Reconciling Management Theory with Management Practice." *Business Horizons* 20 (February 1977):38-47. **Managerial functions.**

A sensible critique of organization and management theory that ignores what managers actually do. A useful complement to Mintzberg's, Woodward's, and Sayles's work.

Schermerhorn, John R. "Determinants of Interorganizational Cooperation." *Academy of Management Journal* 18 (December 1975):846-56. **Organizational communication, Organizational effectiveness.**

A confused attempt at precision in identifying "variables" affecting the organizational proclivity to cooperate.

Scott, William G. "Organization Theory: An Overview and an Appraisal." *Academy of Management Journal* 4 (April 1961):7-26.

An ambitious title but not much content. See his reassessment in 1974.

———. "Organization Theory: A Reassessment." *Academy of Management Journal* 17 (June 1974):242-54.

No better than his earlier piece in 1961.

Shamir, Boas. "Between Bureaucracy and Hospitality: Some Organizational Characteristics of Hotels." *Journal of Management Studies* 15 (October 1978):285-307. **Management policy, strategy, and style, Contingency theory.**

A fascinating study of hotel organization and management. The author's empirical work in this much-neglected area of study reveals some theoretical shortcomings in the most popular literature. **Recommended.**

Simon, Herbert A. *The Shape of Automation for Men and Management.* New York: Harper and Row, 1965. **Decision theory.**

These essays are integrated into his *New Science of Management Decision.*

———. *The Sciences of the Artificial.* Cambridge, Mass.: The M.I.T. Press, 1969. **Decision theory.**

A very difficult book, not because it is hard to understand, but because it is packed with ideas that would require volumes to explore. Stimulating, but be prepared to work at unpacking Simon's thoughts.

———. *Administrative Behavior: A Study of Decision-Making Processes in Administrative Organizations.* 3d ed. New York: Free Press, 1976. **Decision theory, Economic analysis.**

Simon's masterwork. This book includes the ideas that led to his Nobel Prize in 1978 and is one of the best single works in the field. **Highly recommended.**

———. *The New Science of Management Decision.* Rev. ed. Englewood Cliffs, N.J.: Prentice-Hall, 1977. **Decision theory, Economic analysis.**

A collection of revised material published earlier in *The Shape of Automation for Men and Management* and elsewhere. Simon's essays range over the entire field of decisionmaking and include some comment on the computer's role in decisionmaking. **Highly recommended.**

Smith, H. R., and Carroll, Archie B. "Is There Anything 'New' in Management? A 'Rip Van Winkle' Perspective." *Academy of Management Review* (July 1978), pp. 670-74. **Organizational growth and change.**

A quick review of "progress" in organization and management theory. There is not enough detail to be really useful, but it is a good try.

Thompson, James D. *Organizations in Action*. New York: McGraw-Hill, 1967. **Organizational behavior, Managerial functions.**

One of the best books ever on organizations and management. Thompson's work does not provide answers, but he does ask the most intelligent questions. **Highly recommended.**

Thompson, Victor A. *Bureaucracy and the Modern World*. Morristown, N.J.: General Learning Press, 1976. **Bureaucracy, Organizational behavior.**

A brilliant collection of essays whose full research potential has not yet been exploited. Thompson's article on "Organizations as Systems" is particularly noteworthy. **Highly recommended.**

―――. *Modern Organization*. 2d. ed. University: University of Alabama Press, 1977. **Bureaucracy, Organizational behavior.**

Thompson has synthesized many different theoretical ideas into a scholarly text. This book first appeared in 1961 and has been reissued in paperback. **Highly recommended.**

Urwick, L. F. "Why the So-Called 'Classicists' Endure." *Management International Review* 2 (1971):3-14. **Management history, Management policy, strategy, and style.**

An interesting defense of classic administrative thinking by one of the classicists. Urwick gives us some interesting insights into the history of the field.

―――. "That Word 'Organization'." *Academy of Management Review* 1 (January 1976):89-92. **Management history, Organizational design.**

The classicist continues to comment on our organizations.

van de Ven, Andrew H. "A Framework for Organization Assessment." *Academy of Management Review* 1 (January 1976):64-78. **Organizational structure, Organizational behavior.**

An academic, jargonistic exercise with little practical utility.

―――, and Delbecq, André L. "Design Variations within Organizations."

Academy of Management Proceedings (1973), pp. 483-89. **Organizational design, Organizational structure.**

A short piece, loaded with jargon to the point of incomprehensibility. The authors seem preoccupied with attaching new labels to old concepts.

Whitsett, David A. "Making Sense of Management Theories." *Personnel* 52 (May-June 1975):44-52. **Personnel management, Management history.**

A summary of modern human relations management theory. The focus is on contributions of the "big names." This is fairly good primer on the subject.

Woodward, Joan. "Management and Technology." Department of Scientific and Industrial Research. Problems of Progress in Industry No. 3. London: Her Majesty's Stationery Office, 1958. **Organizational growth and change, Management history.**

An excellent examination of organization, production systems, and human relationships in British industry, circa 1953-57. A classic. **Recommended.**

ORGANIZATIONAL BEHAVIOR

Kanter, Rosabeth Moss, and Stein, Barry A., eds. *Life in Organizations.* New York: Basic Books, 1979. **Organizational communication, Organizational effectiveness.**

This is more than an excellent collection of essays on aspects of organizational life. The editors have provided a fine introduction and integrating essays. They present a view of real-life in organizations, and a guide to study for researchers. **Recommended.**

Lansley, Peter; Sadler, Philip; and Webb, Terry. "Organization Structure, Management Style and Company Performance." *Omega* 2 (1974):467-85. **Management policy, strategy, and style, Organizational structure.**

Another interesting study from the U.K. The authors conclude that judgment and uncertainty are big elements in organizational performance. Pure correlation results, but worth a look.

Pfeffer, Jeffrey. "Beyond Management and the Worker: The Institutional Function of Management." *Academy of Management Review* 1 (April 1976):36-46. **Managerial functions, Organization and management theory.**

A review of the potential for institutional cooperation between organizations and its implications for management.

Tushman, Michael L. "A Political Approach to Organizations: A Review and Rationale." *Academy of Management Review* 2 (April 1977):206-16. **Organization and management theory, Decision analysis.**

A literature review with nothing new or helpful.

ORGANIZATIONAL COMMUNICATION

Allen, T. Harrel. "Communication Networks: The Hidden Organizational Chart." *Personnel Administrator* 21 (September 1976):31-35. **Organization and management theory, Information systems.**

An attempt to outline a formal method of mapping informal communicative patterns. The networks exist, but it is questionable whether the networking system presented in the article can successfully map them.

Aram, John D. "Innovation via R&D Underground." *Research Management* 16 (November 1973):24-26. **Innovation, Information systems.**

A good examination of informal (unplanned) communications in R&D organizations. The author argues that a control orientation is not conducive to innovation.

Merrell, V. Dallas. "Huddling to Get Results." *Supervisory Management* 24 (July 1979):3-8. **Managerial functions.**

The author is busily turning a normal managerial practice into a gimmick. His attempts to formalize the process are bound to encounter problems.

Muchinsky, Paul M. "Organizational Communication: Relationships to Organizational Climate and Job Satisfaction." *Academy of Management Journal* 20 (December 1977):592-607. **Personnel management, Organizational psychology.**

A methodological exercise with a great deal of statistical manipulation, but little or nothing useful for managers.

ORGANIZATIONAL CONFLICT

Albanese, Robert. "Overcoming Resistance to Stability." *Business Horizons* 13 (April 1970):35-42. **Organization and management theory, Decisionmaking.**

An intelligent, but overdrawn argument for the positive value of resisting organizational change. The author is against novelty unless it has a purpose.

Bayat, G. R., and Longbottom, D. A. "An Approach to Decision Making in Situations with Conflicting Objectives." *Managerial Finance* 3 (1977): 43-52. **Decisionmaking, Organizational objectives.**

Pure formalistic gibberish. Anyone who has ever dealt with real conflicting objectives will recognize the inanity of this piece.

Lourenco, Susan V., and Glidewell, John C. "A Dialectical Analysis of Organizational Conflict." *Administrative Science Quarterly* 20 (December 1975):489-508. **Manager and controller roles, Managerial functions.**

A fascinating study of central efforts to control field activities in broadcasting, this article describes and analyzes conflict escalation and resolution. **Recommended.**

Schelling, Thomas C. *The Strategy of Conflict: Prospectus for a Reorientation of Game Theory.* Cambridge, Mass.: Harvard University Press, 1963. **Bargaining and negotiation, Systems theory.**

The masterwork of one of the best of the RAND alumni. Schelling brings a rare intelligence to bear on the systematic process of negotiation. The focus is on global conflict (hot and cold), but the utility of the ideas is boundless. **Recommended.**

ORGANIZATIONAL DESIGN

Ackoff, R. L. "Towards Flexible Organizations: A Multidimensional Design." *Omega* 5 (1977):649-62. **Organization and management theory, Planning.**

A scheme for organizational design, similar to "matrix organizations" (see organizational development). Rather confusing and difficult to envision in practice.

Allen, Robert F., and Pilnick, Saul. "Confronting the Shadow Organization: How to Detect and Defeat Negative Norms." *Organizational Dynamics* 2 (Spring 1973):3-18. **Organization and management theory, Organizational conflict.**

An outstanding negative example. This article combines a utopian hyper-control mode with a boy-scout approach to organizational problems with no analytic context.

Ansoff, H. I., and Brandenburg, R. G. "A Language for Organization Design." *Management Science* 17 (August 1971):B705-31. **Decisionmaking, Operations research and management science.**

Much too long, but a useful outline of various organizational design strategies. The author takes a typical formal management science approach to organizational questions.

Burack, E. H., and Negandhi, A. R., eds. *Organization Design: Theoretical Perspectives and Empirical Findings.* Kent, Ohio: Comparative Administration Research Institute, Kent State University, 1977. **Organization and management theory, Organizational growth and change.**

Another collection of essays of varying utility. Nothing new is advanced or discussed. A good overview and nothing more (or less).

Davis, Keith. "Trends in Organizational Design." *Academy of Management Proceedings* (1973), pp. 1-6. **Organization and management theory, Manager and controller roles.**

A short, rather cursory literature review. Davis gives us nothing new, though the article is well-done and captures some of the dominant themes in the organization and management literature.

De Greene, Kenyon B. "Organizational Best Fit: Survival, Change, and Adaptation." *Organization and Administrative Sciences* 8 (Spring 1977):117-33. **Organizational growth and change, Organization and management theory.**

An over-long but interesting survey of organizational adaptation. There are some good points on the interplay of structure, problems, and available technology.

Dowling, William F. "Consensus Management at Graphic Controls." *Organizational Dynamics* 6 (Winter 1977):23-47. **Decisionmaking, Manager and controller roles.**

A long, sometimes tedious case. Some management "lessons" are developed, but they are a bit trite.

Etzioni, Amitai. "An Engineer-Social Science Team at Work." *Research Management* 19 (January 1976):18-22. **Organizational communication, Organizational effectiveness.**

A report of a research center's attempt at electronically linking research group members to retain the dynamics of personal interaction. An interesting experiment.

Farrell, Jack W. "Distribution Organization: Responsibilities in Transition." *Traffic Management* 17 (November 1978):28-39. **Organizational effectiveness, Organizational growth and change.**

Though focused on organizational physical distribution systems, the article provides an informed perspective on adaptability, flexibility, and organizational change.

Galbraith, Jay. *Designing Complex Organizations.* Reading, Mass.: Addison-Wesley, 1973. **Organization and management theory, Organizational growth and change.**

A short book (150 pp.) that has some interesting views of organization, knowledge, and uncertainty. A number of alternative organizing strategies are proposed and discussed.

————. "Organization Design: An Information Processing View." *Interfaces* 4 (May 1974):28-36. **Information processing, Management models.**

A conceptual summary that provides a basic explanation of the author's concept of "matrix organization." **Recommended.**

————. *Organization Design.* Reading, Mass.: Addison-Wesley, 1977. **Organization and management theory, Organizational growth and change.**

This is an extension of Galbraith's earlier work on organizational design. Some of the concepts and arrangements have received wide attention—matrix organizations, for example—so Galbraith's work is worth a look.

Khandwalla, Pradip N. "Viable and Effective Organizational Designs of Firms." *Academy of Management Journal* 16 (September 1973):481-95. **Organizational effectiveness, Organizational structure, Decision analysis.**

A tentative examination of 79 manufacturing firms to determine the association between uncertainty, differentiation, and integration. Some good points.

Lorsch, Jay W. "Organization Design: A Situational Perspective." *Organizational Dynamics* 6 (Autumn 1977):2-14. **Contingency theory, Organization and management theory.**

An intelligent appraisal of organizational task environments. Lorsch is a leading figure in contingency (or situational) theory.

McCaskey, Michael B. "An Introduction to Organizational Design." *California Management Review* 17 (Winter 1974):13-20. **Contingency theory, Organization and management theory.**

Although there is nothing new in this article, it does serve as an adequate primer on contingency views of organization.

Robey, Daniel. "Information Technology and Organization Design." *University of Michigan Business Review* 28 (September 1976):17-22. **Organizational growth and change, Information management.**

A literature review of little interest, even to academic researchers.

Sadler, Philip. "Designing an Organization Structure: A Behavioral Science Approach." *Management International Review* 11 (1971):19-33. **Organizational structure, Organizational growth and change.**

A sensible examination of organizations as decision structures in decision situations.

Shull, F. A., Jr., and Judd, R. J. "Matrix Organizations and Control Systems." *Management International Review* 11 (1971):65-73. **Contingency theory, Control systems and techniques.**

Full of jargon and devoid of meaning or utility.

Weick, Karl E. "Organization Design: Organizations as Self-Designing Systems." *Organizational Dynamics* 6 (Autumn 1977):31-46. **Organizational learning.**

An interesting argument for loosely coupled organizational systems. Not very original, but bright and worthwhile.

Youker, Robert. "Organization Alternatives for Project Management." *Management Review* 66 (November 1977):46-53. **Organization and management theory, Project management.**

A formalistic discussion of matrix organization and project management. This article could be used as a basic primer.

ORGANIZATIONAL DEVELOPMENT

Cahn, Meyer Michael. "Organization Development in the United States Army: An Interview with Lt. Col. Ramon A. Nadal." *Journal of Applied Behavioral Science* 14 (November 1978):523-36. **Organizational design, Contingency theory.**

Organization Development (OD) in the Army. If it wasn't so sad it would be funny: The military operates on the myth of hierarchy, the use of rules, and the power of informal networks. OD applications in the Army deserve serious investigation, not shallow interviews.

Cohen, Stanley L., and Turney, John R. "Intervening at the Bottom: Organizational Development with Enlisted Personnel in an Army Work-Setting." *Personnel Psychology* 31 (1978):715-30. **Organizational design, Contingency theory.**

Organization Development in the Army again. This is a report of an experiment in job satisfaction with low-level enlisted personnel.

Cooper, Cary L., ed. *Organizational Development in the UK and USA: A Joint Evaluation.* New York: Macmillan, 1977. **Comparative management.**

International developments in Organization Development. Only if you're very interested.

Harvey, Jerry B. "Organizations as Phrog Farms." *Organizational Dynamics* 5 (Spring 1977):15-23.

It's sometimes funny, but hardly worth the trouble.

Hornstein, Harvey A., and Tichy, Noel M. "Developing Organization

Development for Multinational Corporations." *Columbia Journal of World Business* 11 (Summer 1976):124-37. **Contingency theory, Analytical methods.**

Organization Development in the multinational corporation. Nothing new.

McGill, Michael M. "Assessing the Effectiveness of Organization Development (OD) Programs." *Organization and Administrative Sciences* 7 (Spring-Summer 1976):123-28. **Contingency theory, Managerial functions.**

Some fuzzy thinking on Organization Development evaluation with some evidence that we don't know whether or not it works.

Patten, Thomas H., Jr., and Dorey, Lester E. "Long-Range Results of a Team Building OD Effort." *Public Personnel Management* 6 (January-February 1977):31-50. **Management policy, strategy, and style, Organizational effectiveness.**

The authors report on the marvels wrought by their OD workshop. This is not research, and it certainly has nothing to do with "long-range" results.

Porras, Jerry I., and Berg, P. O. "The Impact of Organization Development." *Academy of Management Review* 3 (April 1978):249-66. **Organizational growth and change, Organization and management theory.**

A good examination of Organization Development's impact on organizations and individuals. The authors conclude that Organization Development has little effect on anything.

Schein, Virginia E., and Greiner, Larry E. "Can Organization Development Be Fine Tuned to Bureaucracies?" *Organizational Dynamics* 5 (Winter 1977):48-61. **Contingency theory, Organizational design.**

A "contingency" version of Organization Development. The focus is on organizational pathologies that can be treated (fine-tuned?) with the authors' prescription.

Strauss, George. "Organizational Development: Credits and Debits." *Organizational Dynamics* 2 (Winter 1973):2-19. **Organizational growth and change.**

A good primer on Organization Development (OD), although the author overstates the utility of what is essentially a fad.

Tichy, Noel M. "Current Trends in Organizational Change." *Columbia Journal of World Business* 11 (Spring 1974):98-111. **Organizational growth and change.**

Organization Development as an ill-defined solution to everything. This is a good primer, although classical personnel management is similar and more familiar.

White, Bernard J., and Ramsey, V. Jean. "Some Unintended Consequences of 'Top Down' Organization Development." *Human Resource Management* 17 (Summer 1978):7-14. **Hierarchy, Consultants.**

A challenge to conventional wisdom on the installation of Organization Development (OD). For OD believers and researchers.

Wright, Norman H., Jr. "Matrix Management: A Primer for the Administrative Manager." *Management Review* 68 (April 1979):58-61. **Organizational design, Contingency theory.**

First in a series on matrix organization. An adequate primer if the concept is new to you.

ORGANIZATIONAL EFFECTIVENESS

Hitt, Michael; Middlemist, R. Dennis; and Greer, Charles R. "Sunset Legislation and the Measurement of Effectiveness." *Public Personnel Management* 6 (May-June 1977):188-93. **Management in public organizations, Evaluation and program effectiveness.**

A trivial review of the evaluative aspects of sunset legislation.

Steers, Richard M. "When Is an Organization Effective? A Process Approach to Understanding Effectiveness." *Organizational Dynamics* 5 (Autumn 1976):50-63. **Organizational goals and objectives, Organizational psychology.**

An examination of effectiveness as goal realization minus the organizational and individual costs in optimizing. Interesting, but not particularly original.

Wahba, Mahmoud A., and Shapiro, Harris J. "Managerial Assessment of Organizational Components." *Academy of Management Journal* 16 (June 1973):277-84. **Organizational structure, Management models.**

A not particularly useful or insightful listing exercise of management perceptions of organizational effectiveness.

Wildavsky, Aaron. "The Political Economy of Efficiency: Cost-Benefit Analysis, Systems Analysis, and Program Budgeting." *Public Administration Review* 26 (December 1966):292-310. **Cost-benefit analysis, Systems analysis.**

A good, early critique of the approaches Wildavsky has gone on to treat in more detail.

ORGANIZATIONAL GOALS AND OBJECTIVES

Eilon, Samuel. "Goals and Constraints." *Journal of Management Studies* 8 (October 1971):292-303. **Organization and management theory, Performance appraisal.**

A discussion and analysis of *optimal* and *satisficing* organizational goals and strategies.

Frank, Andrew G. "Goal Ambiguity and Conflicting Standards: An Approach to the Study of Organization." *Human Organization* 17 (Winter 1958-59):8-13. **Organizational conflict, Comparative management.**

An early examination of goal ambiguity and conflict in Soviet industrial organizations. Enlightening.

Ivancevich, John M. et al. "Goal Setting: The Tenneco Approach to Personnel Development and Management Effectiveness." *Organizational Dynamics* 6 (Winter 1978):58-80. **Management education and training, Management by objectives.**

A preliminary evaluation of a fancy MBO program (performance planning and evaluation—PP&E) in a conglomerate. Too early to tell much.

Latham, Gary P., and Yukl, Gary A. "A Review of Research on the Application of Goal Setting in Organizations." *Academy of Management Journal* 18 (December 1975):824-45. **Management by objectives, Personnel management.**

A critique of various goal-setting strategies. Conclusion: More research is needed.

Warner, W. Keith, and Havens, A. Eugene. "Goal Displacement and the Intangibility of Organizational Goals." *Administrative Science Quarterly* 12 (March 1968):539-55. **Organizational goals and objectives, Organizational effectiveness.**

A call for clearer goals, measurement of attainment, and specific means-ends chains. Overspecification in some circumstances could be an invitation to disaster, yet context is not part of the authors' analysis.

ORGANIZATIONAL GROWTH AND CHANGE

Daft, Richard L. "A Dual-Core Model of Organizational Innovation." *Academy of Management Journal* 21 (June 1978):193-210. **Innovation.**

An interesting empirical study of innovation in a public school system. The author's dual-core model (technical and administrative) is helpful and warrants further research.

Dunn, William N., and Swierczek, Fredric W. "Planned Organizational Change: Toward Grounded Theory." *Journal of Applied Behavioral Sci-*

ence 13 (1977):135-57. **Administrative reform, Organization and management theory.**

An interesting examination of 11 hypotheses developed from theories of organizational change. The empirical evidence shows only weak support for three.

Hutchinson, John. "Evolving Organizational Forms." *Columbia Journal of World Business* 11 (Summer 1976):48-58. **Organizational design, Organizational structure.**

A formalistic discussion of organizational structure, tasks, and innovation.

Labovitz, George H. "Organizing for Adaptation." *Business Horizons* 14 (June 1971):19-26. **Organizational design, Organizational development.**

Another argument to "do good things." How and when?

Segev, Eli. "How to Use Environmental Analysis in Strategy Making." *Management Review* 66 (March 1977):4-13. **Analytical methods.**

A confusing prescriptive piece. I am not quite sure what the author expects of managers or of his technique.

ORGANIZATIONAL LEARNING

Adams, Sam. "Vietnam Cover-Up: Playing War with Numbers." *Harper's* 250 (May 1975):41-73. **Organizational conflict.**

A fascinating account of how U.S. intelligence agencies refused to use their own legitimate information.

Argyris, Chris. "Double Loop Learning in Organizations." *Harvard Business Review* 55 (September-October 1977):115-25. **Organizational psychology, Organizational design.**

The master of prescriptive organizational psychology not at his best. Argyris offers complicated "models" of organizational learning based on the actors' individual psychological dispositions.

Bandura, Albert. "Behavior Theory and the Models of Man." *American Psychologist* 29 (December 1974):859-69. **Information processing, Organizational behavior.**

Implications of behaviorism and conditioning on individual and organizational learning and innovation.

Bonoma, Thomas V., and Slevin, Dennis P. "Management and the Type II Error." *Business Horizons* 21 (August 1978):61-67. **Decision analysis, Management models.**

An interesting exercise in error diagnosis. The argument is not well developed, but the ideas are suggestive.

Duncan, Robert B. "Toward an Operant Model of Organizational Learning: Adaptation to Environmental Uncertainty." *Academy of Management Proceedings* 32 (1972):155-58. **Decision theory, Risk and uncertainty.**

A thin discussion of adaptive organizational decisionmaking strategies. See Duncan's later article (1974) for more substance and utility.

————. "Modifications in Decision Structure in Adapting to the Environment: Some Implications for Organizational Learning." *Decision Sciences* 5 (October 1974):705-25. **Decision theory, Risk and uncertainty.**

Similar to the author's earlier work (1971-73), this article adds some statistical analysis of an organization's ability to adapt different decisionmaking strategies to changing circumstances over time.

Duncan, W. Jack. "The Knowledge Utilization Process in Management and Organization." *Academy of Management Journal* 15 (September 1972):273-87. **Management education and training, Management policy, strategy, and style.**

Another list of what should and should not be done in putting knowledge to use. A number of new terms are used, but no new ground is broken.

Epps, Garrett. "The Last Days of Skylab." *Washington Post Magazine* (8 April 1979), pp. 10-17. **Cost-benefit analysis, Long-range planning.**

A good account of the effect of cost-effectiveness techniques on NASA's well-publicized Skylab debacle. There is some sobering information on the consequences of ignoring the potential for error in uncertain domains.

Exton, William, Jr. "Treating Errors Like Rejects." *Journal of Systems Management* 28 (June 1977):21-23. **Electronic data processing, Information systems.**

A short (too short) comparison of the techniques needed to detect and correct errors in manufacturing and data management.

Goldfarb, Robert S. "Learning in Government Programs and the Usefulness of Cost-Benefit Analysis: Lessons from Manpower and Urban Renewal History." *Policy Sciences* 6 (1975):281-99. **Cost-benefit analysis, Policy analysis.**

An interesting discussion of the potential for organizational learning within the existing procedures for program design and evaluation. Goldfarb makes a good case for experimental or "learn by doing" approaches to social programs.

Goldner, Fred H. et al. "The Production of Cynical Knowledge in Organizations." *American Sociological Review* 42 (August 1977):539-51. **Organizational effectiveness.**

The role of altruistic motives and "real" behavior in organizations. The example used is the Roman Catholic Church. Interesting.

Jundt, John E.; Ostrom, Lonnie L.; and Schlacter, John L. "Closing the Technology Transfer Gap." *Akron Business and Economic Review* 7 (Fall 1976):21-27. **Research and development, Organizational growth and change.**

Rather obtuse and of questionable utility. The authors discuss moving from innovation to marketing.

Kaufman, Herbert. *Administrative Feedback: Monitoring Subordinates' Behavior.* Washington, D.C.: Brookings Institution, 1973. **Information processing.**

In this engaging book, Kaufman provides a clear outline of the organizational and managerial imperatives of information flows and usage.

Kolb, David A. "Management and the Learning Process." *California Management Review* 18 (Spring 1976):21-31. **Managerial functions, Management policy, strategy, and style.**

The author argues that there is evidence that variations in cognitive style affect the variability of managerial work (see Rosemary Stewart). Communication between the various management styles may also be difficult, which leads Kolb to question universal management "principles."

Landau, Martin. "On the Concept of a Self-Correcting Organization." *Public Administration Review* 33 (November-December 1973):533-42. **Organization and management theory, Management in public organizations.**

An examination of the theoretical potential for self-directed organizational error detection and correction. Some very useful ideas here. **Recommended.**

Nirenberg, John. "Managing Failure." *Supervisory Management* 24 (June 1979):17-22. **Decision models, Management policy, strategy, and style.**

A simplistic, prescriptive statement on error detection and correction.

Post, James E., and Mellis, Marilyn. "Corporate Responsiveness and Organizational Learning." *California Management Review* 20 (Spring 1978):57-63.

Corporate responses to social pressures are discussed, but it is hard to tell why.

Steele, F. I. "Organizational Overlearning." *Journal of Management Studies* 9 (October 1972):303-14. **Organizational goals and objectives.**

A good discussion of organizational overspecialization, or trained incompetence.

Warmington, Allan. "Obsolescence as an Organizational Phenomenon." *Journal of Management Studies* 11 (October 1974):96-114. **Problem solving.**

A good article on organizational error detection and correction. The author discusses diagnoses, i.e., problem identification and analyses.

ORGANIZATIONAL PSYCHOLOGY

Back, Kurt W. *Beyond Words: The Story of Sensitivity Training and the Encounter Movement.* New York: Russell Sage Foundation, 1972. **Management education and training, Personnel management.**

An extensive, critical study of sensitivity training and the encounter movement. This is one of the few systematic examinations of the modern move to "self-actualization" and organizations.

Katz, Daniel, and Kahn, Robert L. *The Social Psychology of Organizations.* New York: John Wiley, 1966. **Organization and management theory, Management models.**

A very influential and often cited text. The authors' point of view crops up again and again in other work done in the late 1960s and early 1970s.

Leavitt, Harold J., and Pondy, Louis R., eds. *Readings in Managerial Psychology.* 2d ed. Chicago: University of Chicago Press, 1973. **Managerial functions, Organization and management theory.**

An excellent collection. The editors keep revisions up-to-date without sacrificing worth to fashion. **Recommended.**

Miller, Jon. "Isolation in Organizations: Alienation from Authority, Control, and Expressive Relations." *Administrative Science Quarterly* 20 (June 1975):260-71. **Organizational design.**

A survey of attitudes and perceptions in several small-scale organizations. It is not clear, however, what the findings mean.

Orpen, Christopher, and Nkohande, Joshua. "Self-Esteem, Internal-Control and Expectancy Beliefs of White and Black Managers in South Africa." *Journal of Management Studies* 14 (May 1977):193-99. **Organizational effectiveness, Comparative management.**

Once-over-lightly on perceptions of low-level managers. A correlational study that does not explain much.

Slovic, Paul, and Fischoff, Baruch. "On the Psychology of Experimental Surprises." *Journal of Experimental Psychology* 3 (1977):544-51. **Managerial functions, Organizational psychology.**

Psychological experiments that hint at explaining why so many useless management control systems are adopted and retained. We tend to believe what we want to believe or what we are told, especially when results are presented as scientific, despite evidence to the contrary.

Weick, Karl E. *The Social Psychology of Organizing.* Reading, Mass.: Addison-Wesley, 1969. **Organization and management theory, Analytical methods.**

A short book, but with a wide-ranging discussion of organizations, their environments, and their members. The author is able to touch on a number of conceptual issues without losing the focus on organizational structure and practices.

ORGANIZATIONAL STRUCTURE

Cummings, L. L., and Berger, Chris J. "Organization Structure: How Does It Influence Attitudes and Performance?" *Organizational Dynamics* 5 (Autumn 1976):34-49. **Organizational design, Organization and management theory.**

A survey of studies of organizational structure. The authors conclude that the evidence is mixed and more research is needed. There are some interesting observations on how little we do know about organizations and management.

Davis, Stanley M. "Two Models of Organization: Unity of Command Versus Balance of Power." *Sloan Management Review* 16 (Fall 1974):29-40. **Organizational design, Decision analysis.**

A good discussion of decision structures and organizational politics. Davis recommends *managing* rather than solving most problems. **Recommended.**

Kakabadse, Andrew. "Organization Structure and Attitudes to Work: An Assessment of Social Service Departments." *Management Decision* 17 (1979):189-201. **Policy analysis, Administrative reform.**

A look at formal organizational structure and its attendant problems. The author recommends flexibility and an emphasis on problem solving.

Reimann, Bernard C. "Dimensions of Structure in Effective Organizations: Some Empirical Evidence." *Academy of Management Journal* 17 (December 1974):693-708. **Organizational effectiveness, Evaluation and program effectiveness.**

A straight correlational study with no new ideas or suggestions.

Terry, Pat. "The Organization of Management." *Management Today* (July-December 1977), pp. 107-108. **Managerial functions.**

A rather thin offering with a plea for understanding or influencing the organization's environment. Terry gives us no help on how or why.

Webber, Ross A. "Staying Organized." *Wharton Magazine* 3 (Spring 1979):16-23. **Redundancy, Management policy, strategy, and style.**

A good, sensible statement on pragmatic duplication and overlap in five major corporations: General Motors, General Electric, International Telephone and Telegraph, Johnson & Johnson, and Liberty Mutual Insurance.

REDUNDANCY

Hage, Jerald. "A Strategy for Creating Interdependent Delivery Systems to Meet Complex Needs." *Organization and Administrative Sciences* 5 (Spring 1974):17-37. **Evaluation and program effectiveness, Policy analysis.**

The author sketches a strategy of using intermediate organizations to provide duplication and overlap—a critical element in social welfare delivery systems—but he does not seem aware of the concepts, since he criticizes duplication along the way.

Landau, Martin. "Redundancy, Rationality, and the Problem of Duplication and Overlap." *Public Administration Review* 29 (July-August 1969):346-58. **Organization and management theory.**

The seminal statement on the positive application of redundancy to organizations. Landau gives us an antidote to the poison of the "efficient" model. **Highly recommended.**

RESEARCH AND DEVELOPMENT

Baer, Walter S.; Johnson, L. L.; and Merrow, E. W. "Government-Sponsored Demonstrations of New Technologies." *Science* 196 (May 1977):950-57. **Technology transfer, Risk and uncertainty.**

A good discussion of private/public agency collaboration in demonstration projects in technically uncertain domains. There are some interesting conclusions on who bears the costs.

Beard, Edmund. *Developing the ICBM.* New York: Columbia University Press, 1976. **Organizational growth and change, Organizational learning.**

A study of the organizational factors in the Air Force's ICBM development program. Again, the technological problems proved somewhat easier to handle than the struggles between traditional "bomber men" and the proponents of the ballistic missile.

Bujake, John E., Jr. "Ten Myths About New Product Development." *Research Management* 15 (January 1972):33-42. **Innovation.**

An interesting essay on the interplay of demand and innovation. The argument could well be extended to the continuous invention and subsequent discard of new management tools and techniques.

Emme, Eugene M., ed. *History of Rocket Technology: Essays on Research, Development and Utility.* Detroit: Wayne State University Press, 1964. **Organizational growth and change.**

An insightful collection with some interesting views on how research and development programs *really* work.

Flinn, P. A., and Bolling, G. F. "Is There an Objective Way to Spend Corporate Moneys on Scientific Research?" *Research Management* 13 (January 1970):63-74. **Decision analysis, Analytical methods.**

The authors assume or define away obstacles and proceed to develop their model. Very neat, but unworkable for obvious reasons.

Gambino, Anthony J., and Gartenberg, Morris. "The Management of Research and Development." *Management Accounting* 60 (November 1978):58-59. **Control systems and techniques.**

A research report summary. Efforts are underway to control corporate research and development activities, with mixed success.

Gee, Robert E. "A Survey of Current Project Selection Practices." *Research Management* 14 (September 1971):38-45. **Project management, Decisionmaking.**

A short but interesting analysis of corporate research and development (R&D) project selection criteria and the decisionmaking process. Finding: Most R&D efforts are intended to support existing business.

Globe, Samuel et al. "Key Factors and Events in the Innovation Process." *Research Management* 16 (July 1973):8-15. **Innovation, Planning.**

An enlightening report of a study on innovation and the potential for controlling research and development activities. **Recommended.**

Gunz, Hugh P., and Pearson, Alan. "How to Manage Control Conflicts in Project Based Organizations." *Research Management* 22 (March 1979): 23-29. **Project management, Organizational conflict.**

A discussion of types of organizational conflict in research and development units, with various management strategies suggested. Prescriptive and formal.

Hunt, Raymond G., and Rubin, Ira S. "Approaches to Managerial Control in Interpenetrating Systems: The Case of Government-Industry Relations." *Academy of Management Journal* 16 (June 1973):296-311. **Organizational communication, Organizational behavior.**

An interesting examination of the pragmatic political interaction between government and industry in research and development projects. There are some useful general lessons.

Lasser, Marvin E. "Management Update: The Army Science and Technology Program." *Defense Systems Management Review* 3 (Autumn 1978):47-53. **Decentralization.**

Research and development (R&D) in the army. Facing the same problems as all organizations in matching R&D to requirements, the Army develops a set of guidelines. There is nothing on how well they work.

Long, T. P. "Laser Processing: From Development to Application." *Research Management* 19 (January 1976):15-17. **Innovation.**

A short case study of the progress from discovery to process. This article is worth reading for its insights on how knowledge is gained and applied—a key managerial function.

Merrifield, Bruce. "Industrial Project Selection and Management." *Industrial Marketing Management* 7 (October 1978):324-30. **Information management, Project management.**

The author explores the need to exploit the "surprise factor" in converting innovations into marketable products. There is not much on how this is to be done.

Moore, R. F. "Five Ways to Bridge the Gap Between R&D and Production." *Research Management* 13 (September 1970):367-73.

A formal process statement of little or no practical use.

Paolillo, Joseph G., and Brown, Warren B. "How Organizational Factors Affect R&D Innovation." *Research Management* 21 (March 1978):12-15. **Innovation, Organizational design.**

A report of a study that reinforces an argument for reducing hierarchic control of research and development units.

Rechtin, Eberhardt. "It Was an R&D Success, but the Project Died." *Vital Speeches of the Day* 46 (April 1978):400-404. **Project management.**

An engineer's view of government, rationality, and design. Rechtin provides an interesting perspective that is not common in the profession.

Rickover, Admiral H. G. *The Role of Engineering in the Navy.* Washington D.C.: U.S. Department of the Navy, 1974.

This is useful because it represents the views of perhaps the single most influential individual in U.S. defense policy in the past 30 years.

Roberts, Edward B. "Facts and Folklore in Research and Development Management." *Industrial Management Review* 8 (Spring 1967):5-18. **Management education and training, Decisionmaking.**

A reasoned view of research and development management and the myths that surround decisionmaking and activities in this domain.

Servi, I. S. "Information Transfer—Handle with Care." *Research Management* 19 (January 1976):10-14. **Information management, Management information systems.**

An interesting argument that questions the process and hardware emphasis that is found in most discussions of information transfer. Short and a bit jargonistic, but useful.

Specht, R. D. "RAND: A Personal View of Its History." *Operations Research* 8 (December 1960):825-39. **Systems analysis, Operations research and management science.**

A fascinating account of the beginning of perhaps the most successful R&D organization in the world. There are some good organizational lessons on problem solving and decisionmaking.

SUPERIOR-SUBORDINATE RELATIONSHIP

Franklin, Jerome L. "Down the Organization: Influence Processes Across Levels of Hierarchy." *Administrative Science Quarterly* 20 (June 1975):153-64. **Managerial functions, Hierarchy.**

A technical study of linkages across hierarchical levels. Highly abstract and probably of interest only to researchers.

Hrebiniak, Lawrence G. "Job Technology, Supervision, and Work-Group Structure." *Administrative Science Quarterly* 19 (September 1974):395-410. **Organizational structure, Organizational design.**

A short study of organizational structure, job technology, and degrees of supervisory control. The article generally affirms earlier studies indicating that control varies with technology.

Kanter, Rosabeth Moss. "Power Failure in Management Circuits." *Harvard Business Review* 57 (July-August 1979):65-74. **Organizational structure.**

An excellent examination of the awkward role of middle management and first-line supervisors. There is some element of "responsibility without authority" in the article, but it goes beyond that cliché.

Marcus, Philip M., and House, James S. "Exchange Between Superiors and Subordinates in Large Organizations." *Administrative Science Quarterly* 18 (1973):209-22. **Personnel management, Managerial functions.**

An examination of several hypotheses from human relations and Weberian theory. The results are suggestive rather than conclusive, but the article is interesting nonetheless.

Planning and Policy

LONG-RANGE PLANNING

Carper, William B.; Barton, Frank M., Jr.; and Wunder, Haroldene F. "The Future of Forecasting." *Management Accounting* 61 (August 1979):27-31. **Management accounting, Analytical methods.**

A survey of financial analysts' attitudes toward information sources and disclosure. Formal statements are ranked low. The authors propose more formalisms (forecasting) as an alternative.

Carroll, Archie B., and Kefalas, Asterios G. "The Impact of Environmental Protection on Organization and Decision-Making." *Managerial Planning* 27 (March-April 1979):27-34. **Organizational growth and change, Decisionmaking.**

A cursory discussion of environmental protection regulations on corporate decisionmaking and organization.

Fildes, Robert; Jalland, Mike; and Wood, Doug. "Forecasting in Conditions of Uncertainty." *Long Range Planning* 11 (August 1978):29-38. **Risk and uncertainty.**

Some good points are buried in this argument for forecasting and the need for user/preparer overlap (matrix), with the user a more active participant in forecasting.

Kallman, Ernest A., and Gupta, Rakesh C. "Top Management Commitment to Strategic Planning: An Empirical Study." *Managerial Planning* 27 (May-June 1979):34-38. **Planning, Management policy, strategy, and style.**

The authors argue that long-term planning is most often used when uncertainty is high. They then explain that motor freight firms do not plan because of high uncertainty. Confusing, but interesting.

Lindsey, Bradford A. "Forecasting for Control." *Management Accounting* 58 (September 1976):41. **Control systems and techniques, Organizational learning.**

An account of how one manufacturing firm (apparel) uses past events as a basis for market and production forecasts. This is a very simple approach that requires long-term experience to evaluate accuracy.

Naor, Jacob. "Planning by Consensus: A Participative Approach to Planning." *SAM Advanced Management Journal* 43 (Autumn 1978):40-47. **Organizational growth and change, Planning.**

An argument for planning by permanent committees. There is no explanation of *how* this is to be done.

Rue, Leslie W., and Fulmer, Robert M. "Is Long-Range Planning Profitable?" *Academy of Management Proceedings* 33 (1973):66-73. **Planning, Management accounting.**

Some interesting information on the success *and* failure of long-range (3-5 years) planning in industry, measured in accounting terms.

Said, Kamal E., and Seiler, Robert E. "An Empirical Study of Long-Range Planning Systems: Strengths-Weaknesses-Outlook." *Managerial Planning* 28 (July-August 1979):24-28. **Control systems and techniques, Analytical methods.**

A report of a survey of planners: Top management support is a problem.

Thackray, John. "How U.S. Planners Came Unstuck." *Management Today* (UK) (January 1977), pp. 44-46. **Organizational growth and change.**

A short but informative rundown of long-range planning in some major U.S. corporations.

PLANNING

Ackoff, Russell. "A Concept of Corporate Planning." *Long Range Planning* 3 (September 1970):2-8. **Decisionmaking.**

In this frustrating article, the author attempts a succinct description of planning, but winds up in obfuscation and rationalizations of the inadequacies of formal, optimizing strategies.

Austin, John E. "Computer-Aided Planning and Decision Making in the U.S.S.R." *Datamation* 23 (December 1977):71-74. **Computer services, Bureaucracy.**

Illustrates the preoccupation of Soviet planners with centralization and control. There is no evaluation of the system's effectiveness.

Bould, Sally. "Rural Poverty and Economic Development: Lessons from the

War on Poverty." *Journal of Applied Behavioral Science* 13 (1977):471-88. **Economic development, Management in public organizations.**

A useful essay that recognizes the political character of social welfare programs.

Brown, Arnold. "When the Planner Speaks, Does Management Really Listen?" *Management Review* 67 (November 1978):58-61. **Decisionmaking, Organizational communication.**

Another complaint about the plight of the planner: No one listens.

Devons, Ely. *Planning in Practice: Essays in Aircraft Planning in War-Time.* Cambridge, England: Cambridge University Press, 1950. **Organization and management theory, Manager and controller roles.**

A collection of marvelous essays on planning, this book should be required reading for all planners. **Recommended.**

Faulkner, John C. "Strategic Plans: Made to Be Broken?" *Management Review* 68 (April 1979):21-25. **Organizational growth and change.**

Another shallow plea for the imperative need for organizational planning.

Friedmann, John. *Retracking America.* Garden City, N.Y.: Doubleday, 1973. **Policy analysis.**

In one of the better books on planning, Friedmann brings a great deal of experience to bear in this extended essay. This is a wide-ranging discussion with a number of specific recommendations, and includes a select annotated bibliography.

Galloway, Thomas D., and Mahayni, Riad G. "Planning Theory in Retrospect: The Process of Paradigm Change." *Journal of the American Institute of Planners* 43 (January 1977):62-71. **Organization and management theory, Analytical methods.**

The authors try to apply Thomas Kuhn's model to planning theory, and not very successfully. A good bibliography, but not much else.

Gilbert, Xavier, and Lorange, Peter. "Five Pillars for Your Planning." *European Business*, no. 41 (Autumn 1974), pp. 57-63. **Management policy, strategy, and style, Decision models.**

A vacuous statement, this article illustrates the pervasive misunderstanding of management behavior. The authors ignore the mismatch of "principles" and practice identified by Herbert A. Simon in the 1940s.

Holmberg, Stevan R. "Regional Planning Regulation in the United States." *Long Range Planning* 11 (October 1978):72-77. **Long-range planning.**

Another treatise on planning that tells us nothing.

Irwin, Patrick H. "Who Really Believes in Strategic Planning?" *Managerial Planning* 27 (November-December 1978):6-9.

Platitudes, clichés, and chestnuts.

Jerstad, Finn E. "An Administrator's Manual of Planning." *Planning Review* 4 (September 1976):13. **Manager and controller roles, Management policy, strategy, and style.**

A suggested rulebook that becomes a pointless exercise.

Johnson, Michael L. "Strategic Planning: Is That What You're Doing?" *Industry Week* 199 (27 November 1978):94-97. **Management policy, strategy, and style, Organizational goals and objectives.**

Interviews with executives explaining how and why they do strategic planning. But are they really doing it? Who knows?

Kaplan, Abraham. "On the Strategy of Social Planning." *Policy Sciences* 4 (1973):41-61.

A discussion of the pitfalls in planning as end rather than means. Kaplan's comment on "Scientism" vs. scientific method makes this worth reading.

Kirby, M. J. L., and Kroeker, H. V. "The Politics of Crisis Management in Government: Does Planning Make Any Difference?" *Journal of Business Administration* 9 (Spring 1978):179-95. **Management in public organizations.**

The Canadian experience with government planning in the 1970s. Informative.

Knoepfel, Rudolph W. "The Politics of Planning: Man in the Decision Process." *Long Range Planning* 6 (March 1973):17-21. **Policy analysis.**

A fascinating mixture of realism (politics in planning) and a plea for clear goals and psychologizing—treating the planner as hero. Interesting.

McCaskey, Michael B. "A Contingency Approach to Planning: Planning with Goals and Planning without Goals." *Academy of Management Journal* 17 (June 1974):281-91. **Organizational goals and objectives, Contingency theory.**

An interesting discussion of goal setting and formal, rational planning strategies.

Moore, Terry. "Why Allow Planners to Do What They Do? A Justification from Economic Theory." *Journal of the American Institute of Planners* 44 (October 1978):387-97. **Policy analysis, Economic analysis.**

Planning and the economic theory of public goods are outlined and explained. This is intended as a justification for planning, but it doesn't quite work.

Naylor, Thomas H. "The State of the Art of Planning Models." *Planning Review* 4 (November 1976):22-27. **Modeling and simulation.**

A report of a 1975 symposium on corporate planning models. Arguments for and against are presented, though somewhat sketchily.

Pennington, Malcolm W. "Why Has Planning Failed?" *Long Range Planning* 5 (March 1972):2-9. **Managerial functions.**

An anecdotal discussion of planning that is long on prescription and short on evidence.

Ringbakk, Kjell A. "Why Planning Fails." *European Business,* no. 28 (Spring 1971), pp. 15-27. **Organizational effectiveness, Organizational learning.**

A useless list of "dos and don'ts" with an exhortation not to do dumb things.

Sayles, Leonard. "Technological Innovation and the Planning Process." *Organizational Dynamics* 2 (Summer 1973):68-80. **Managerial functions, Innovation.**

A good summary of Sayles's views. The author has conducted a number of empirical studies, and this statement includes points on redundancy, premature programming, and other organizational patterns.

Sepulveda, Claudio R. "Systemic Health Planning." *Long Range Planning* 12 (June 1979):62-72.

Systems, health, and planning. Nothing new, just some rearranged labels and concepts.

Taylor, Bernard. "Introducing Strategic Management." *Long Range Planning* 6 (September 1973):34-38. **Management education and training, Decisionmaking.**

An example of education as an answer to all management planning problems. Taylor assumes that because there are problems with strategic planning, there should be a graduate program in it. Left unanswered are the questions of what is to be taught in such programs.

Wagle, B. "Management Science and Strategic Planning." *Long Range Planning* 3 (April 1971):26-33. **Operations research and management science, Modeling and simulation.**

A very formal, process-oriented article that contributes little to our understanding of the use of management science and planning in organizations.

Wildavsky, Aaron. "If Planning Is Everything, Maybe It's Nothing." *Policy Sciences* 4 (1973):127-53. **Control systems and techniques, Policy analysis.**

A polemic by a master polemicist, this article is often considered the definitive critique of comprehensive, formally rational planning. **Recommended.**

POLICY ANALYSIS

Brewer, Garry D. *Politicians, Bureaucrats, and the Consultant: A Critique of Urban Problem Solving.* New York: Basic Books, 1973. **Consultants, Computer services.**

An excellent study of the interplay of policy and formal decision models in major U.S. cities. One of the best treatments of this very difficult area. **Recommended.**

Halperin, Morton H. *Bureaucratic Politics and Foreign Policy.* Washington, D.C.: Brookings Institution, 1974. **Management in public organizations.**

A fascinating account of the *real* policymaking process. As Halperin points out, policymaking is not at all like the formal, rational models provided by most theorists.

Heclo, Hugh. *A Government of Strangers.* Washington, D.C.: Brookings Institution, 1977. **Bureaucracy.**

An interesting study of the constant maneuvering of career bureaucrats and political appointees in government. Heclo uses information provided by the participants in an analysis of the tactics used to either gain control (appointees) or maintain continuity (career officials).

Lazarsfeld, Paul F. "The Policy Science Movement (An Outsider's View)." *Policy Science* 6 (September 1975):211-22. **Systems approach.**

A sensible critique by one of the pioneers in applied social research. Short and useful, if you are interested in the field.

Orlans, Harold. "Neutrality and Advocacy in Policy Research." *Policy Sciences* 6 (1975):107-19.

A diffuse discussion of objectivity in policy research in particular and the social sciences in general.

Park, Rolla Edward. "The Role of Analysis in the Formation of Cable Television Regulatory Policy." *Policy Sciences* 5 (1974):71-81. **Policymaking, Analytical methods.**

A short summary of the real uses to which analysis is put in policymaking. There are no surprises for managers, but some enlightening discussion for preachers of formalisms.

Sapolsky, Harvey M. "Science Policy." In *Handbook of Political Science,* edited by Fred I. Greenstein and Nelson Polsby. Reading, Mass.: Addison-Wesley, 1975, pp. 79-110. **Analytical methods.**

A penetrating and incisive review of policies and opportunities in science and technology. The author also examines the role of science in developing and evaluating public policy.

Schulman, Paul R. "The Reflexive Organization: On Decisions, Boundaries and the Policy Process." *Journal of Politics* 38 (November 1976):1014-23. **Organization and management theory, Decision models.**

A model of organizational response to its environment. Short and sketchy.

Smith, Thomas B. "The Policy Implementation Process." *Policy Sciences* 4 (1973):197-209. **Developing countries.**

A tentative move toward an explanatory model of implementation. There is some utility in the author's treatment of tensions in implementation.

Steinbruner, John D. *The Cybernetic Theory of Decision.* Princeton, N.J.: Princeton University Press, 1974. **Decision theory, Control systems and techniques.**

A dense and difficult book that applies cybernetic principles to arms control and nuclear proliferation. Using cybernetics and psychology to analyze organizational decision is a sticky area (Ross Ashby and Stafford Beer do it), and does not always clarify the decisionmaking process.

van Meter, Donald S., and van Horn, Carl E. "The Policy Implementation Process: A Conceptual Framework." *Administration and Society* 6 (February 1975):445-88. **Policymaking.**

Long and boring literature review; a good update with little synthesis.

Vesper, Karl H., and Sayeki, Yutaka. "A Quantitative Approach for Policy Analysis." *California Management Review* 15 (Spring 1973):119-26. **Organizational control, Organizational goals and objectives.**

An example of the spurious precision attached to problem-solving approaches based on mathematical manipulation.

Wildavsky, Aaron. *Speaking Truth to Power: The Art and Craft of Policy Analysis.* Boston: Little, Brown, 1979. **Policymaking, Management in public organizations.**

So far, this is *the* definitive book on policy analysis. The writing is lucid, intelligent, and informed. Wildavsky at his best. You cannot understand the education of analysts or the practice of policy analysis without having read this book. **Recommended.**

POLICYMAKING

Abert, James G. "Defining the Policy-Making Function in Government: An Organizational and Management Approach." *Policy Sciences* 5 (1974): 245-55. **Organization and management theory, Management in public organizations.**

A definitional exercise with not much practical use; but it does reflect the confusion and imprecision of most efforts at "policy analysis."

Bunker, Douglas R. "Policy Sciences Perspectives on Implementation Processes." *Policy Sciences* 3 (1972):71-80.

An example of academic obscurity. The author's conceptual confusion is surpassed only by the impossibly jargonistic language.

Horowitz, Irving Louis. "Social Science Mandarins: Policymaking as a Political Formula." *Policy Sciences* 1 (1970):339-60.

A critique of past activities of social scientists in formulating and implementing social policies. There are some good points buried in polemics.

Sapolsky, Harvey M. "A Solution to the Health Crisis." *Policy Analysis* 3 (Winter 1977):115-21.

A short discussion of some simple methods for dealing with health care problems in the U.S.

Winthrop, Henry. "Social Systems and Social Complexity in Relation to Interdisciplinary Policymaking and Planning." *Policy Sciences* 3 (1972):405-20. **Systems analysis, Information systems.**

Grand computer simulations and their application to models of planning. A case is made for "counterintuitive" policy. This is a jumbled argument with an abundance of jargon.

Vickers, Geoffrey. "Values, Norms and Policies." *Policy Sciences* 4 (1973):103-11. **Control systems and techniques, Policy analysis.**

A neat essay on the ability of any system to respond to control measures that are taken to correct cybernetic mismatch signals. The role of changing norms in defining what is and is not considered mismatch is discussed.

Woolsey, R. E. D. (Gene)

Short and polemical, Woolsey's articles in *Interfaces* and other journals should be required reading for all OR/MS professionals and those who employ them. He always overstates and often oversimplifies, but he never obfuscates, unlike others in his profession. You do not have to agree with Woolsey to realize that what he is saying needs saying, and may well produce some improvement in the services provided by OR/MS practitioners.

"A Candle to Saint Jude, Of Four Real World Applications of Integer Programming." *Interfaces* 2 (February 1972):20-27.

"Operations Research and Management Science Today, Or Does an Education in Checkers Really Prepare One for a Life of Chess?" *Operations Research* 20 (May-June 1972):729-37.

"A Novena to St. Jude, Or Four Edifying Case Studies in Mathematical Programming." *Interfaces* 4 (November 1973):32-39.

"O Tempora, O Mores, O C. Jackson Grayson, Jr." *Interfaces* 4 (May 1974):76-78.

"Homage to W. A. C. Bennette and the Canadian Operations Research Society, Or 'Entia non Sunt Multiplicanda Praeter Necessitatem'." *Interfaces* 4 (August 1974):43-46.

"Some Reflections on Surviving as an Internal Consultant, Azerbaijan, and Two Thieves." *Interfaces* 5 (November 1974):48-52.

"The Measure of M.S./O.R. Applications, Or Let's Hear It for the Bean Counters." *Interfaces* 5 (February 1975):74-78.

"On Doing Good Things and Dumb Things in Production and Inventory Control." *Interfaces* 5 (May 1975):65-67.

"Rules for Consulting Survival: A Biased View." *Interfaces* 5 (August 1975):66-68.

"Three Short Studies in Industrial Psychology: Time, Don Juan and Motivation." *Interfaces* 6 (November 1975):44-46.

"On Doing Operations Research in the Cracks, Or if the Error Isn't Within, It Must Be Between." *Interfaces* 6 (February 1976):42-44.

"Reflections on the Past of Scientific Management and the Future of Management Science." *Interfaces* 6 (May 1976):3-4.

"A Triennial Editorial Policy." *Interfaces* 6 (August 1976):3-6.

"Three Digressions on the Routing of Trucks: Ice and Snow, Garbage and More Garbage." *Interfaces* 7 (November 1976):18-21.

"Two Digressions on Systems Analysis: Optimum Warehousing and Disappearing Orange Juice." *Interfaces* 7 (February 1977):17-20.

"The Warehouse Model That Couldn't Be and the Inventory That Couldn't Be Zero." *Interfaces* 7 (May 1977):14-17.

"How to Succeed as an Internal Consultant, Or It's Not How That Matters, But When!" *Interfaces* 7 (May 1977):15-17.

"A Case of Optimum Trucking, Or to Keep on Rising, Just Keep on Truckin'." *Interfaces* 8 (November 1977):12-15.

"Walking thru Warehouses, Toolcribs and Shops, Or Profits thru Peripatetics." *Interfaces* 8 (February 1978):15-20.

"Prolegomena on Promoting Practice, Or Pecksniff, Gotz von Berlichingen, Symptoms and Reality." *Interfaces* 8 (May 1978):7-12.

"An Essay on Misused Words: Sophisticated and Elegant and on Going Thataway with MIS." *Interfaces* 8 (August 1978):12-15.

"Two OR/MS Detective Stories: The Shrapneled Shed and the Disappearing Product." *Interfaces* 9 (February 1979):8-12.

"An Exemplary Essay on Communication or Corporate Style, Corporate Substance, and the Sting." *Interfaces* 9 (May 1979):10-12.

"Whatever Happened to Simple Simulation? A Question and an Answer." *Interfaces* 9 (August 1979):9-11.

"Two Essays on Model Motivation: With this Sign, Optimize and the Shekels of Silver Solution." *Interfaces* 9 (November 1979):13-17.

With Gulley, David A. "You Can *Too* Use Operations Research." *Health Services Research* 8 (Summer 1973):97-101.

Name Index

Abbas, M.B.A., 91
Abernathy, William J., 135
Abert, James G., 169
Acker, Joan, 129
Ackoff, Russell L., 17, 19, 25, 39, 146, 164
Adamolekun, 'Lapido, 83
Adams, Carl R., 39
Adams, Sam, 153
Adedeji, Abebayo, 92
Akpala, Agwu, 92
Albanese, Robert, 145
Albrecht, Karl, 105
Aldrich, Howard, 132
Alexander, Ernest R., 65
Allen, Robert F., 146
Allen, T. Harrel, 145
Allison, Graham T., 66
Alter, Steven L., 40
Altman, Steve, 67
Anderson, Donald N., 7
Anderson, John C., 17
Anderson, Lane K., 110
Anderson, Scarvia B., 94
Anderson, William J., 122
Ansoff, H.I., 146
Anthony, Robert N., 8, 53, 110
Anthony, William P., 112
Aplin, John C., Jr., 106
Aram, John D., 91, 145
Arbib, Michael A., 34

Archer, Earnest R., 129
Archer, John F., 109
Archibald, K.A., 26
Argentima, John, 122
Argyris, Chris, 39, 40, 114, 153
Armstrong, J. Scott, 16
Arnoff, E. Leonard, 19
Aronofsky, Julius S., 72
Arrow, Kenneth J., 16, 136, 137
Ashby, Ross, 169
Assmus, Gert, 66
Atherton, Judith, 74
Atherton, Roger M., 20, 114
Austin, John E., 164
Austin, Nancy K., 96
Austin, Vincent, 89
Axelson, Charles F., 38
Axelson, Kenneth S., 53
Azrael, Jeremy R., 100

Baarspul, J.A., 89
Babcock, Richard, 106
Back, Kurt W., 156
Baer, Walter S., 158
Baker, Donald W., 53
Baker, H. Kent, 14
Baker, Ken, 136
Ball, Samuel, 94
Balogun, M.J., 84
Baltz, Gerald W., 137
Ballon, Robert J., 100

Subject Index